W9-DGD-120

Doodle Stitching
EMBROIDERY & BEYOND

Doodle Stitching
EMBROIDERY & BEYOND
CREWEL, CROSS STITCH, SASHIKO & MORE

Aimee Ray

LARK CRAFTS
Asheville

Editor: Amanda Carestio

Art Director: Shannon Yokeley

Graphic Designer: Raquel Joya

Photographer: Cynthia Shaffer

Cover Designer: Raquel Joya

An Imprint of Sterling Publishing
387 Park Avenue South
New York, NY 10016

If you have questions or comments about
this book, please visit: larkcrafts.com

Ray, Aimee, 1976-
    Doodle stitching : embroidery & beyond : traditional techniques made fresh & fun / Aimee Ray. -- First Edition.
      pages cm
    Includes index.
    ISBN 978-1-4547-0363-1 (pbk. : alk. paper)
    1. Embroidery--Patterns. 2. Stitches (Sewing) I. Title.
    TT771.R369 2013
    746.44--dc23
                                    2012022820

10 9 8 7 6 5 4 3 2 1

First Edition

Published by Lark Crafts
An Imprint of Sterling Publishing Co., Inc.
387 Park Avenue South, New York, NY 10016

Text © 2013, Aimee Ray
Photography © 2013, Lark Crafts, An Imprint of Sterling Publishing Co., Inc.
Illustrations © 2013, Aimee Ray

Distributed in Canada by Sterling Publishing,
c/o Canadian Manda Group, 165 Dufferin Street
Toronto, Ontario, Canada M6K 3H6

Distributed in the United Kingdom by GMC Distribution Services,
Castle Place, 166 High Street, Lewes, East Sussex, England BN7 1XU

Distributed in Australia by Capricorn Link (Australia) Pty Ltd.,
P.O. Box 704, Windsor, NSW 2756 Australia

Manufactured in China

ISBN 13: 978-1-4547-0363-1

For information about custom editions, special sales, premium and corporate purchases, please contact
Sterling Special Sales Department at 800-805-5489 or specialsales@sterlingpub.com.

For information about desk and examination copies available to college and university professors, requests
must be submitted to academic@larkbooks.com. Our complete policy can be found at www.larkcrafts.com.

Contents

x x x x x x x x x x x x x x x x x x x x x

Beyond Basic Embroidery...

xxxxxxxxxxxxxxxxxxxxxxxxxxxxxxxxxxxxxxxxxxxxxxxxxxxx

Hand embroidery has always been popular among crafters, and it's easy to see why: embroidery is fun, inexpensive, portable, and versatile. In my first two Doodle Stitching books, I introduced my technique of freestyle hand embroidery with some basic skills and stitches, ideas for easy projects, and tons of motifs for you to use for all of your embroidery endeavors. In this book, I'll take you a step further.

Using basic embroidery skills as a starting point, I'll equip you with new techniques and plenty of ideas to set you off into several new directions. Learn to give new dimensions to your stitching with stumpwork, cutwork, or Shisha. Create a modern geometric design with Sashiko. Add color to your work with paint, crayon tinting, or appliqué. Spice up traditional embroidery projects with funky decorative stitches, or find a new spin on age-old techniques like crewel, redwork, or cross stitch.

In each chapter, you'll find an introduction to the different embroidery techniques followed by instructions for a fun project or two so you can apply what you learned. Here's what you can make:

- Create an art piece for your walls: the **Canvas Cuckoo Clock** has real working clock parts and lovely water-colored birdies.

- Fall in love with cross stitch while whipping up the **Forest Friends Keepsake Quilt**: you decide where your stitched squirrels and foxes live.

- Make a **Merry Mushroom Pincushion**—with dimensional stumpwork toadstools—that you'll love and use.

- Stitch a family heirloom with the colorful and lovely **Crewel Family Tree**.
- Sew a **Candyland Apron** for the little baker in your life—it's fun with appliquéd cupcakes and lollipops.

You'll also find a section full of alternate patterns and templates you can use in place of the ones shown or to create your own projects, including a complete cross-stitch and monogram alphabet (pages 113 and 118).

This book isn't designed to bury you in technical details, but rather to introduce you to several fun embroidery techniques with a simple overview and basic instructions for each one. And just because these techniques go beyond basic embroidery doesn't necessarily mean they're any more difficult. Once you learn a little about each technique, you may find one or two that interest you the most and decide to dive in deeper and learn more about these skills on your own. I've also included basic embroidery instructions and a stitch glossary (page 104) in case you're new to embroidery or need a little refresher course.

I hope you'll have fun, learn something new, and be inspired to take a step beyond basic embroidery!

— Aimee

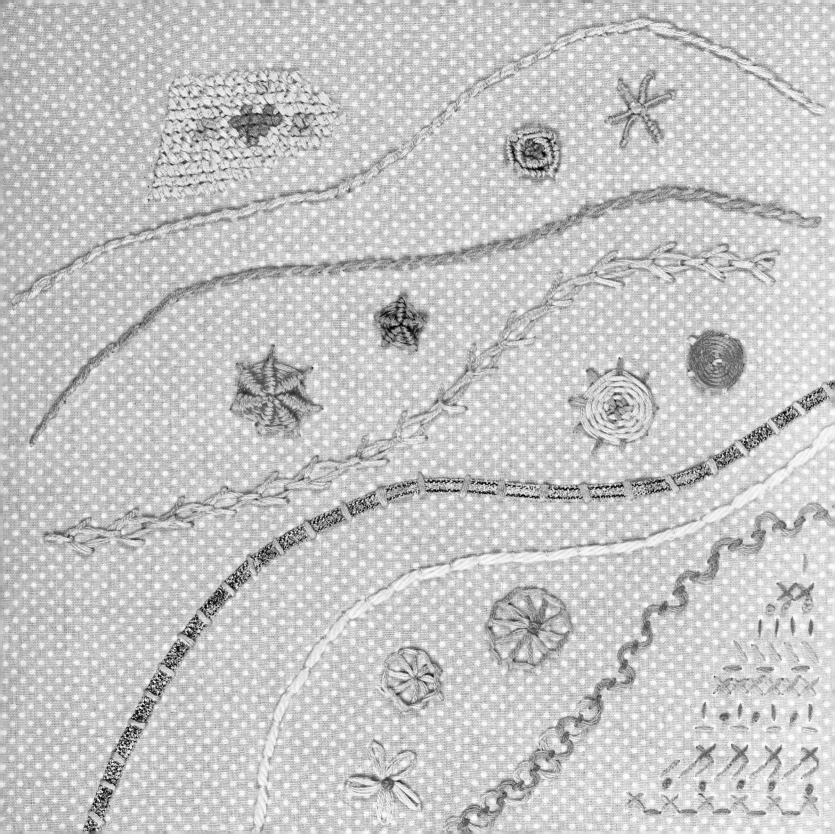

Chapter 1

Cross Stitch & Decorative Stitches

x x x x x x x x x x x x x x x x x x x x x x x x x x x x x x x x x x x x x x x x

You can give your work a whole new feel by experimenting with different kinds of basic and advanced stitches. Cross Stitch is so fun and easy. And who can resist a pair of cross-stitched bibs or a cross-stitched fox on a patchwork baby quilt? Decorative stitches, like the Bullion Knot and the Woven Spider's Wheel, are perfect for creating heirloom pieces like the Monogrammed Handkerchief and for fun little projects like the Zipper Pouch.

Cross Stitch

Cross Stitch is traditionally done on Aida fabric, which has a visible weave that you can use to count your stitches. You can adjust the size of your cross stitches according to the size you want your pattern to be and the size or "count" of the Aida.

Waste canvas is a very loosely woven grid fabric that can be used to create designs on any non-Aida fabric. Simply pin a piece of waste canvas to your fabric, and stitch through the canvas and fabric together, using the grid to count your stitches. When you're done stitching the design, carefully pull out the waste canvas strand by strand.

Cross Stitch designs can also be done without counting but instead stitching crosses in different sizes combined with diagonal, horizontal, and vertical Straight Stitches. This is usually done over a transferred pattern like regular hand embroidery.

Cross Stitch ---------------------------------

Begin by making a Straight Stitch diagonally from A to B. Make another Straight Stitch across the first stitch from C to D. When making a row or solid area of Cross Stitches, keep all the top stitches going in the same direction to make your work look neat and smooth. To make this easier, you can do a row or area of just the underlying stitches, and then go back and cross them all at once.

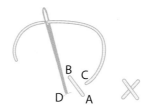

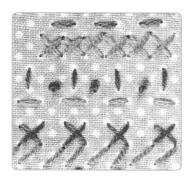

Decorative Stitches

Decorative stitches add a striking dimension to your embroidery projects. Some are simple and some are complex, but all are unique and easy to learn with a bit of practice. Here are a few of my favorites; you'll need to know these to complete the projects that follow.

Bullion Knots

Bullion Knots are similar to French Knots. Start by bringing the needle out of the fabric at A. Make a stitch about ¼ inch (0.6 cm) wide from B to C (close to A). This will be the length of your Bullion Knot. While the end of the needle is sticking out of the fabric, wrap floss around the needle five to seven times. Now slowly pull the needle and floss through the wraps while you hold them down to the fabric with your thumb. Reinsert the needle at A, pulling the coil of wraps tightly to the fabric. Stitch several Bullion Knots pointing out from a center point to make a flower or star shape, or stitch several curving around each other to make Bullion Roses.

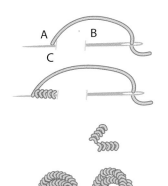

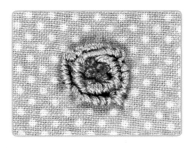

Couching

Couching is stitching a loose strand of floss to the top of your fabric. Simply arrange the floss and make tiny Stab Stitches over it and back through the fabric to hold it down. Make your stitches about ¼ inch (0.6 cm) apart. Use thread of the same color to hide the Stab Stitches or a contrasting color if you want the stitches to stand out. You can use Couching to attach pieces of yarn, ribbon, rickrack, or cords to your fabric as well.

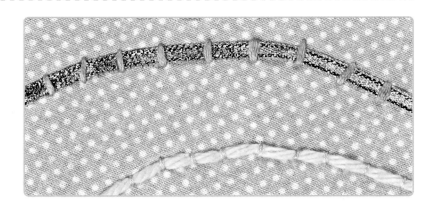

Woven Spider's Wheel

The Woven Spider's Wheel is perfect for stitching circles and flowers. Start by making an odd number of Straight Stitches (usually five or seven) in a star shape out from a center point. Make these spokes about ½ inch (1.3 cm) long or as big as you want your Spider's Wheel to be. Bring your needle and floss up at the center between two spokes and slide them over one stitch and under the next, round and round the circle until you reach the outer ends of the spokes.

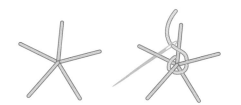

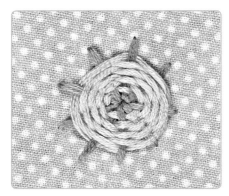

Whipped Spider's Wheel

The Whipped Spider's Wheel is similar to the Woven version, except you'll whip your stitches over each spoke. Start with a Straight Stitched star, then bring your needle and floss up between two spokes. Next take your needle over one spoke and under two spokes. Repeat all around the circle.

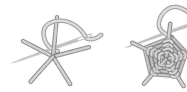
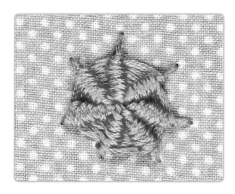

Buttonhole Wheel

A Buttonhole Wheel is stitched like a Buttonhole or Blanket Stitch. Bring the needle up at A, and make a loose stitch from A to B, your center point. Catch the stitch under your needle at C, pulling it tight to the fabric.

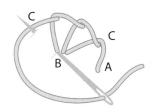
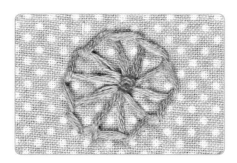

Whipped Stem Stitch

To make a Whipped Stem Stitch, start with a Stem Stitched line and then make diagonal stitches over it in a different color. Slide the needle under the row of Stem Stitches, not through the fabric.

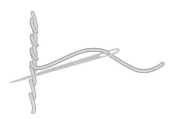

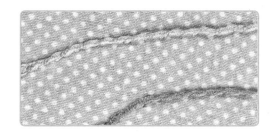

Threaded Fly Stitch

For a Threaded Fly Stitch, start with a line of Fly Stitches, then begin a new piece of floss in a different color at A. Pass the needle and floss under the scallop part (B) and under the straight part (C) of each Fly Stitch (not through the fabric), back and forth down the line. When you reach the end, you can go back in the opposite direction.

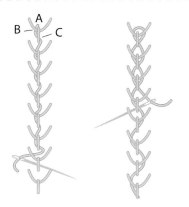

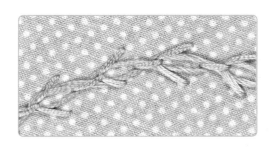

Threaded Running Stitch

To make a Threaded Running Stitch, start with a line of Running Stitches close together. Begin a new color of floss at A, sliding the needle back and forth, under each Running Stitch. You can leave it like this, or begin a third color at A and slide the needle back and forth under the Running Stitches in the opposite direction. At the end of the line, pull the floss through the fabric, but not too tightly, and knot it at the back.

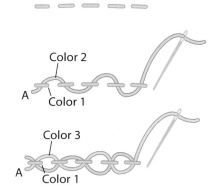

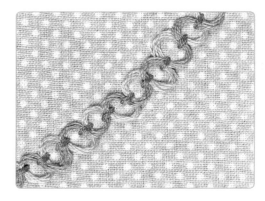

ABCs & 123s Cross Stitch Bibs

× ×

These bibs are sweet and quick to stitch: instead of making one Cross Stitch for every woven square of the fabric, you'll make one over every four squares.

WHAT YOU NEED

One 14-count cotton Aida bib for each Cross Stitch design

Embroidery floss

For ABCs: 1 skein each of coral, light green, and turquoise*

For 123s: 1 skein each of coral, dark coral, light coral, and light green*

For ABCs, the author used DMC embroidery floss colors 352, 472, and 598; for 123s, she used 350, 351, 353, and 472.

STITCHES

Cross Stitch

INSTRUCTIONS

1. Locate the center point of the design (marked by a darkened square on each pattern). Then, find the center point of the bib by folding it in half twice: vertically, then horizontally. This is where you'll make your first stitch.

2. Using all 6 threads of floss, sew Cross Stitches over 4 squares of the Aida, counting the number of crosses for each letter or shape, and working your way through the design.

3. For the row of Xs on the ABCs design, start with one large Cross Stitch over 16 squares of Aida and continue across the line.

ABCs & 123s Cross Stitch Bibs

Note: Each square on this chart represents four squares on your fabric.

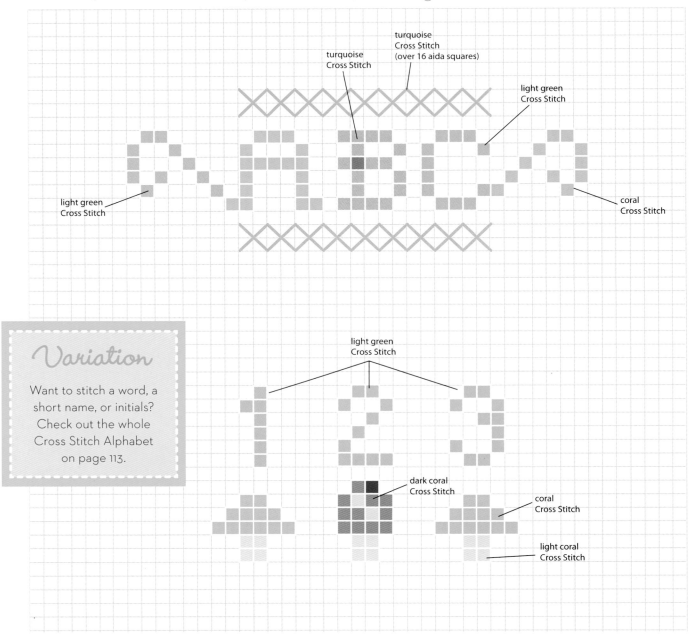

turquoise
Cross Stitch
(over 16 aida squares)

turquoise
Cross Stitch

light green
Cross Stitch

light green
Cross Stitch

coral
Cross Stitch

light green
Cross Stitch

Variation

Want to stitch a word, a short name, or initials? Check out the whole Cross Stitch Alphabet on page 113.

dark coral
Cross Stitch

coral
Cross Stitch

light coral
Cross Stitch

Fair Isle Doll Skirt

××××××××××××××××××××××××××××××××××××

Create an easy "Fair Isle" style pattern using Cross
Stitches in different sizes paired with diagonal, horizontal,
and vertical straight stitches. This little felt skirt can be
easily adjusted to fit almost any 1:6 scale doll.

Fair Isle Doll Skirt

WHAT YOU NEED

Template (below)

Wool blend felt, 7 x 4-inch (17.8 x 10.2 cm) piece for the skirt

8.5-count tear-away waste canvas

Embroidery floss, 1 skein each of light gray, aqua, turquoise, light brown, and brown*

Hook-and-loop tape or small snaps

The author used DMC embroidery floss colors 3024, 3811, 3810, 437, and 420.

STITCHES

Cross Stitch

Straight Stitch

INSTRUCTIONS

1. Trace the skirt template onto the felt. Cut out the skirt. Cut a piece of waste canvas big enough to cover the skirt and pin it in place. You'll stitch through the canvas and felt together, using the grid to count your stitches.

2. Locate the center point of the design (this is marked by a darkened stitch on each pattern). Then, find the center of the skirt by folding it in half. You'll begin stitching at the top row of the pattern.

3. Using 3 of the 6 threads of floss, begin your stitches at the center point and work your way out. Once you have one row finished, you can work row–by–row beneath it.

4. To create the dots, make a tiny Cross Stitch over the intersecting lines of the waste canvas.

5. When you're done stitching the design, carefully pull out the waste canvas strand by strand.

6. Wrap the skirt around your doll and determine where the fasteners need to go. Sew either hook-and-loop tape or snaps in place.

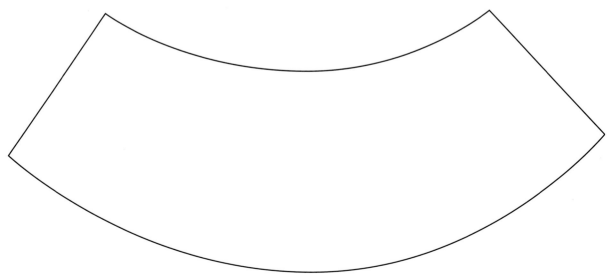

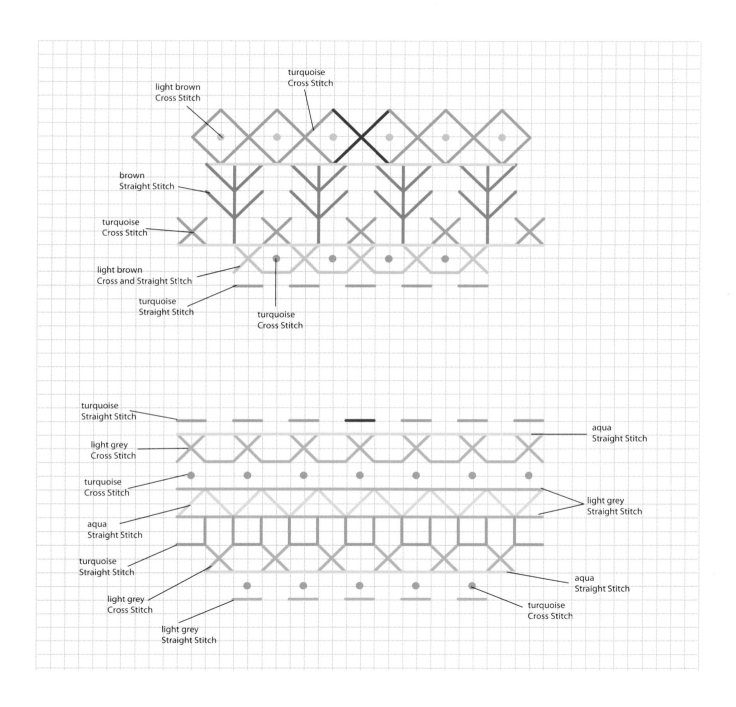

light brown
Cross Stitch

turquoise
Cross Stitch

brown
Straight Stitch

turquoise
Cross Stitch

light brown
Cross and Straight Stitch

turquoise
Straight Stitch

turquoise
Cross Stitch

turquoise
Straight Stitch

light grey
Cross Stitch

turquoise
Cross Stitch

aqua
Straight Stitch

turquoise
Straight Stitch

light grey
Cross Stitch

light grey
Straight Stitch

aqua
Straight Stitch

light grey
Straight Stitch

aqua
Straight Stitch

turquoise
Cross Stitch

Forest Friends Keepsake Quilt

What friends are hiding in your quilted forest? Cross Stitch a bunny, a fox, a host of trees, and more onto a sweet, simple patchwork background. Create a real family heirloom by recycling old fabrics, especially favorite children's clothes.

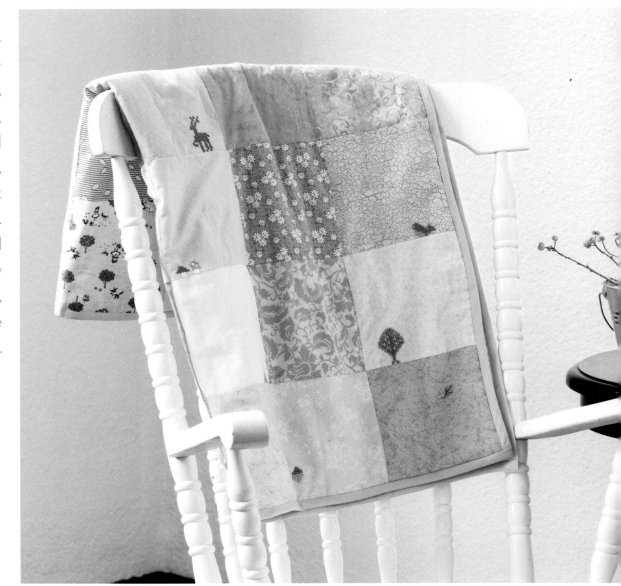

WHAT YOU NEED

36 squares of fabric, 6 inches (15.2 cm)

Embroidery floss, 1 skein each of gray, aqua, light brown, brown, tan, cream, orange, coral red, coral, green, light green, forest green, and light forest green*

8.5-count tear-away waste canvas

1½ yard (1.1 m) of quilt batting

1¼ yard (1.1 m) of fabric for backing, or assorted strips that are 40 inches (101.6 cm) long

Safety pins

6 yards (5.5 m) of double fold bias tape

The author used DMC embroidery floss colors 648, 598, 422, 420, 739, 712, 3853, 350, 352, 472, 471, 368, and 369.

STITCHES

Appliqué Stitch

Cross Stitch

INSTRUCTIONS

1. Arrange the squares in 6 rows across and 6 rows down. Stitch the squares together across each row, then stitch the rows together, lining up the seams as you go.

2. Choose a woodland pattern and a square to stitch it on. Cut a piece of waste canvas and pin it in place. Using all 6 threads of floss, stitch through the canvas and fabric together, using the grid to count your stitches. When you're done stitching the design, carefully pull out the waste canvas, strand by strand.

3. Continue stitching motifs, scattering them throughout the quilt.

4. Measure and cut a piece of batting 2 inches (5.1 cm) larger than the quilt top on all sides. Cut a piece of fabric or sew different fabrics together to make a backing the same size as the batting.

5. Now you'll make the "quilt sandwich." On a large, flat surface, spread out your quilt backing, face down. Spread out the batting on top of the backing, aligning the edges. Center the quilt top, face up, on the batting.

6. Find the center of the quilt and insert a safety pin through all three layers. Moving out from the center, smooth all layers flat and pin them together at every other square or so. Now you can

move the quilt around or hold it in your lap as you finish the quilting.

7. The easiest way to quilt a quilt is to tie the layers together with short lengths of embroidery floss or yarn. Starting in the middle of a square, pass the threaded needle through the layers from bottom to top, then make a small stitch by turning the needle and going back through top to bottom. Tie the floss in a tight double knot and trim the ends to ½ inch (1.3 cm). If you use floss colors to match the squares on the front, you can barely see them.

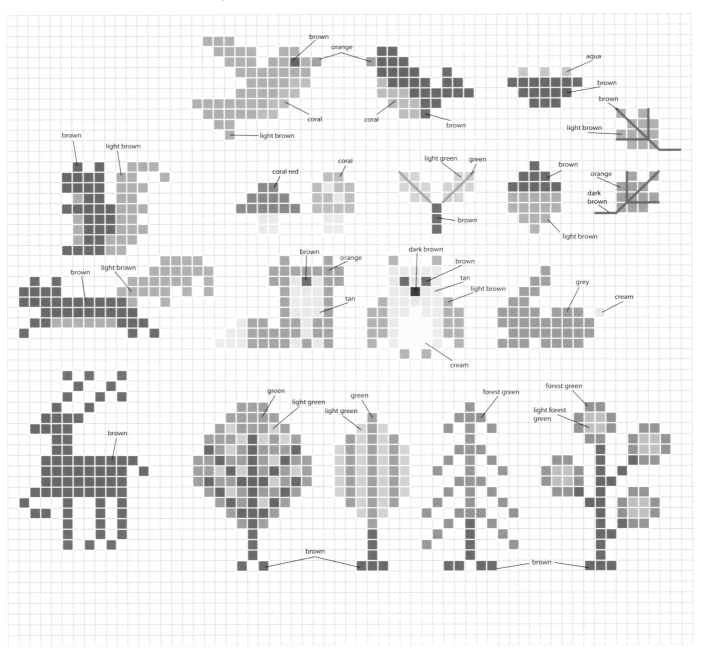

INSTRUCTIONS (CONTINUED)

8. Continue making ties all over the quilt, one in the center of each square, and one at each four-corner cross section. When you finish tying, remove all the safety pins.

9. Cut two pieces of binding 36 inches (91.4 cm) long, and two pieces 39 inches (99.1 cm) long.

10. Unfold a piece of 36-inch (91.4 cm) binding and line up one raw edge with an edge of the quilt top, right sides facing. Pin the binding in place and stitch along the fold nearest the edge. Trim off the extra batting and backing so that the quilt edge is even with the edge of the binding. Fold the binding over the edge of the quilt and attach it to the backing along the narrow folded edge, using the Appliqué Stitch (see page 33). Sew the other 36-inch (91.4 cm) piece of binding to the opposite edge of the quilt in the same way.

11. Unfold a 39-inch (99.1 cm) piece of binding and line it up with one of the remaining sides of the quilt. Allow the ends to hang over both sides of the quilt by 1½ inches (3.8 cm). Sew the binding to the quilt along the edge and trim off the extra batting and backing from this side. Fold under one raw end so it will wrap over the corner when you turn

the binding to the back. Hand-sew that end closed, then continue stitching the binding to the back of the quilt. Stop 2 inches (5.1 cm) from the opposite corner and fold under and stitch the remaining raw edge.

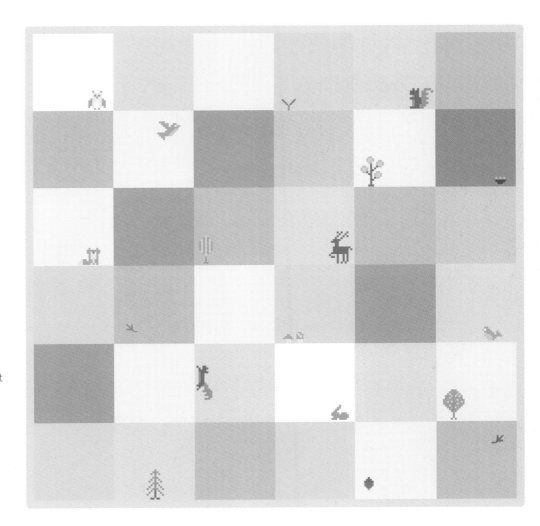

Flower Hill Zipper Pouch

Perfect for lip gloss, small treasures, and maybe even sewing supplies, this sweet little pouch makes a lovely canvas for a colorful hillside covered with flowers.

WHAT YOU NEED

Piece of pink quilter's cotton fabric, 12 x 6 inches (30.5 x 15.2 cm)

Embroidery floss, 1 skein each of light orange, pink, light pink, coral, light coral, green, light green, purple, light purple, turquoise, and aqua*

6-inch (15.2 cm) pieces of blue or green yarn, thin rickrack, and/ or ribbon

4-inch (10.2 cm) pink zipper

The author used DMC embroidery floss colors 3854, 3712, 761, 351, 353, 471, 472, 3835, 211, 597, and 598.

STITCHES

Bullion Knot

Buttonhole Wheel

Couching

French Knot

Satin Stitch

Stem Stitch

Threaded Running Stitch

Threaded Fly Stitch

Whipped Spider's Wheel

Whipped Stem Stitch

Woven Spider's Wheel

INSTRUCTIONS

1. Measure and mark two 4½ x 5-inch (11.4 x 12.7 cm) squares onto the wrong side of the fabric. Add ½ inch (1.3 cm) to each edge for seam allowance. Do not cut out the square yet.

2. Transfer the embroidery pattern onto one of the squares, leaving an extra ½ inch (1.3 cm) of fabric above the design at the top.

3. Embroider the design, and then cut out the squares.

4. Press under the top ½ inch (1.3 cm) of fabric on each square. Pin the folded side of the embroidered square along one side of the zipper and sew it down. You can do this with a machine or hand-sew it with a small, tight back stitch. Sew the folded edge of the remaining square to the other side of the zipper.

5. Unzip the zipper partway, and fold the pouch so it is inside out. Pin the two fabric squares together with right sides facing and sew along the three remaining edges. Trim the corners and snip off any access fabric or zipper ends. Turn the pouch right side out.

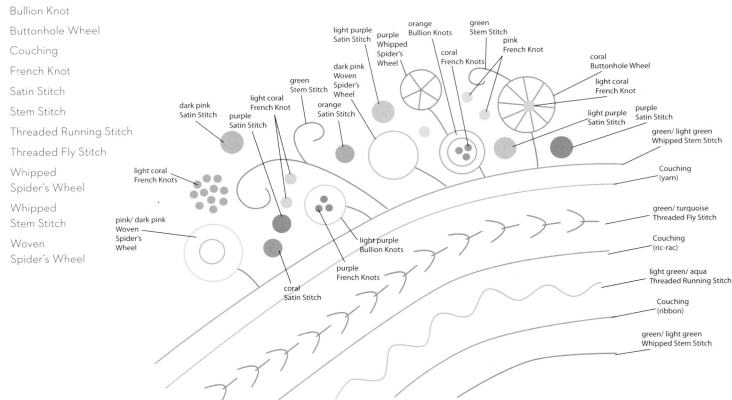

Heirloom Monogrammed Handkerchief

Tea-dying fabric gives it an instant aged look. Add some pretty embroidery, and this handkerchief becomes a special keepsake.

WHAT YOU NEED

White handkerchief
(or white fabric)

Tea

Embroidery floss, 1 skein each of
brown, light brown, turquoise,
and aqua*

*The author used DMC embroidery
floss colors 422, 420, 597, and 598.*

STITCHES

French Knot

Bullion Knot

Satin Stitch

Stem Stitch

INSTRUCTIONS

1. You can make your own handkerchief
by cutting a square of white cotton
fabric and sewing a narrow double-fold
hem on all four sides. Or use a store-
bought or vintage handkerchief.

2. To tea-dye your handkerchief, brew a
cup of strong black or dark tea. Immerse
the fabric in the tea for several minutes.
Rinse out the fabric to check the color;
if you want it to be darker, let it soak
longer in the tea. Let the handkerchief
dry completely.

3. Size the monogram letter as
needed and transfer it onto one
corner of the handkerchief.

4. First sew the Satin Stitch section
of the letter, then outline it with the
Stem Stitch. Make Bullion Knot roses
on each circle, or use any advanced
stitches you like.

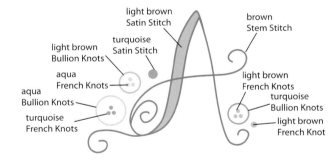

Variation

Check out the complete
Monogram Alphabet on page 118
for more design options.

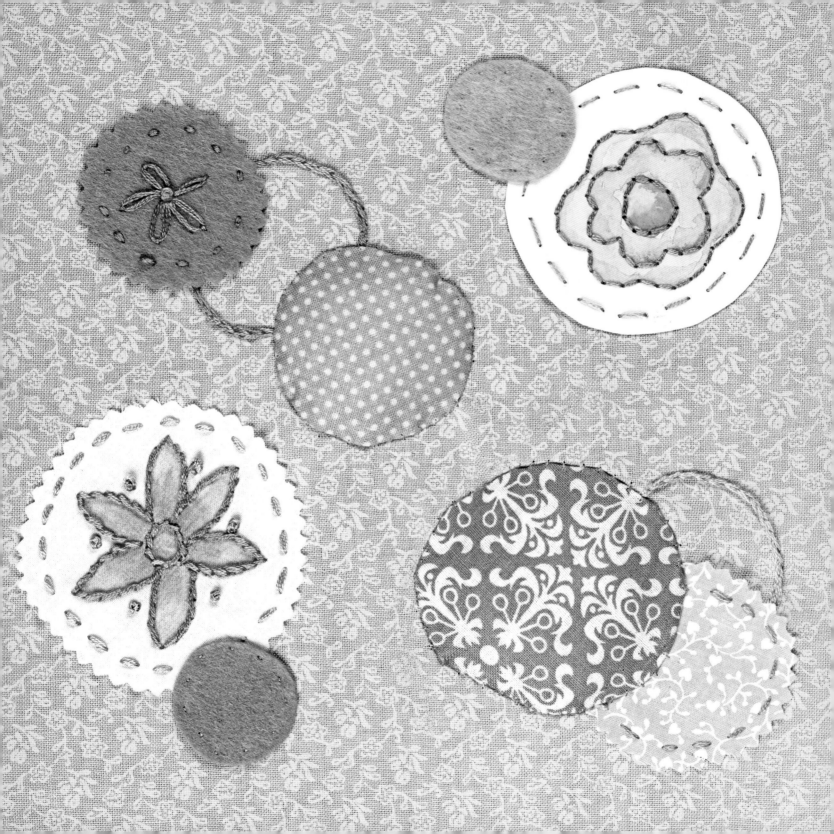

Chapter 2

Appliqué & Color

× ×

Line work embroidery is pretty and fun, but sometimes you want a little extra boost for your projects. It's easy to enhance your embroidery with lots of color by using colored fabrics for appliqué or by painting or crayon tinting your fabric before you stitch. These versatile techniques will add a new dimension to your stitch work.

Adding Color

When embroidering on canvas or paper, try painting or coloring the pattern after you transfer it on, before you begin stitching. Watercolors, crayons, and colored pencils work best. Thicker paints can interfere with your stitching, making it difficult to get your needle through. They may also crack as you try to stitch.

Crayon Tinting

Crayon tinting is easy to do and creates permanent color on fabric. After transferring your pattern to the fabric, place it onto a hard surface and LIGHTLY begin filling in spaces on the pattern with color. Don't press too hard: use very light strokes. Create blends by using more or darker strokes at the center points of each shape and lightening them as you move outward. Next, place your fabric on a towel or ironing board with a piece of white paper on top of it. Iron over the paper on the hottest setting. This will set the color into the fabric and also remove any excess wax. Iron for a few minutes, until no more wax is released onto the paper. You can go back and add more color if you want to, then repeat the ironing step. Now simply embroider the pattern.

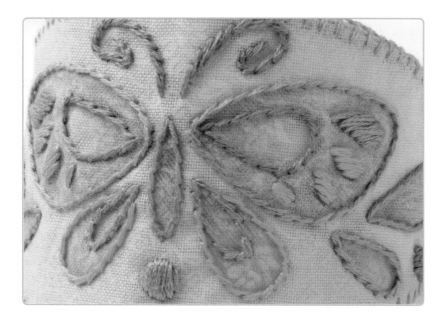

Appliqué

Appliqué is a simple process with a fancy name: essentially, you're stitching one fabric layer on top of another. But there are many variations from that basic definition.

When using cotton or other fabric for appliqués, I use pinking shears for a decorative edge or fold the edges under (you can also use fusible web to adhere your shapes if you'd like). Felt shapes or other fabric shapes cut with pinking shears can be stitched on using any embroidery stitch, most commonly the Stab Stitch (see page 102).

To turn your edges under (and hide fraying fabric edges), draw your shape onto the fabric and cut it out ¼ inch (0.6 cm) beyond the lines. Press the ¼-inch (0.6 cm) seam to the back of the appliqué shape and stitch it on with the Appliqué Stitch; more on that below.

To add dimension to your appliqué as in the Candyland Apron (page 34), create puffy appliqué shapes from cotton fabrics. First cut out the fabric pieces, leaving an extra ½ inch (1.3 cm) around the edges. For each piece, cut a matching piece from white fabric as well. For each shape, pin the color and white

pieces together with right sides facing, and sew around the edge ½ inch (1.3 cm) in, leaving a 1-inch (2.5 cm) opening. Notch around the edges, turn the piece right side out, and press the seams flat. Stuff a tiny bit of stuffing inside to make it puffy, and stitch it in place using the Appliqué Stitch.

Appliqué Stitch

Pin the appliqué shape in place on the fabric background. Pull a knotted length of thread from the back of the background fabric to the front at A, very near the edge, and through the appliqué. Insert the needle back through the background fabric at B and bring the tip of the needle up again at C. Pull the thread tightly through, securing the fabrics together. Continue making even, equally spaced stitches around the perimeter of the appliqué.

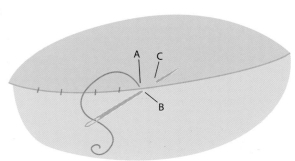

Candyland Apron

x x x x x x x x x x x x x x x x x x x x x x x x x x x x x x x x x x x x x x x

Give your sweet appliqué treats added dimension with this special technique. This apron is child-sized, but you can easily enlarge the design for an adult-sized apron. Better yet, make a matching set.

WHAT YOU NEED

Templates (page 36)

Scraps of light pink, dark pink, yellow, and aqua cotton fabric

Scraps of light pink, dark pink, and aqua wool blend felt

Embroidery floss, 1 skein each of pink, yellow, and aqua*

White fabric

A child-sized, bib-style apron

Stuffing

The author used DMC embroidery floss colors 961, 3855, and 598.

STITCHES

Appliqué Stitch

Back Stitch

Lazy Daisy

Satin Stitch

Split Stitch

Stab Stitch

INSTRUCTIONS

1. Enlarge the appliqué templates 150% (or size to your liking). Trace them onto the felt and fabric, and embroider the designs.

2. Cut out the appliqué shapes, leaving an extra ½ inch (1.3 cm) around the edges. Cut a matching piece from the white fabric as well. Cut out the felt pieces on the template line.

3. For each appliqué shape, pin the color and white pieces together with right sides facing. Stitch around the edge with a ½-inch (1.3 cm) seam allowance, leaving a 1-inch (2.5 cm) opening. Clip the curved edges, turn the piece right side out, and press the seams flat. Leave the opening as it is for now.

4. From a larger piece of aqua fabric, cut a shape for the ground below the candy. Match the bottom edge to the shape of your apron. Pin this piece in place and stitch it on using the Appliqué Stitch.

5. Push a tiny bit of stuffing inside each appliqué shape, then sew it in place on the apron using the Appliqué Stitch, closing the opening as you sew.

6. Position each felt piece on the apron, and sew it down using the Stab Stitch.

7. Embroider the remaining parts of the design (the lollipop "stems" and "leaves").

Candyland Apron

Variation

Switch things up with a forest-themed apron using the extra appliqué patterns on page 110.

Enlarge 150%

dark pink fabric

aqua Satin Stitch

light pink felt

aqua fabric

pink Lazy Daisy

yellow Split Stitch

light pink felt

dark pink fabric

aqua Split Stitch

dark pink felt

pink Satin Stitch

yellow fabric

pink Back Stitch

light pink fabric

aqua felt

yellow Split Stitch

pink Lazy Daisy

light pink fabric

aqua fabric

Felt Appliqué Babushka

×××××××××××××××××××××××××

This cute babushka doll has so much personality. Stitch up a few in different sizes for a whole set of nesting dolls.

Felt Appliqué Babushka

WHAT YOU NEED

Templates (page 39)

1 piece of pink felt, 9 x 12 inches (22.9 x 30.5 cm)

1 piece of lavender felt, 9 x 12 inches (22.9 x 30.5 cm)

Scraps of felt in pink, dark pink, lavender, dark purple, reddish purple, brown, and white

Embroidery floss, 1 skein each of coral, dark coral, white, brown, plum, and light plum*

Stuffing

The author used DMC embroidery floss colors 352, 351, 433, 3835, and 3836.

STITCHES

French Knot

Straight Stitch

Lazy Daisy

Satin Stitch

Split Stitch

Stab Stitch

Whip Stitch

INSTRUCTIONS

1. Enlarge the doll templates 200% (or size to your liking). Trace the templates onto the felt and cut them out.

2. Use the Stab Stitch to secure the felt pieces together:
- Attach the hair to the face, then secure the face in the hood opening.
- Position the apron on top of the skirt opening. Evenly space eight ovals around the curved edge, tucking part of each oval underneath the apron. Secure in place.
- Position the hood with the bottom edge overlapping the skirt. Secure along the overlapped edge.
- Place the remaining pieces according to the stitch pattern.

3. Transfer the embroidery design onto the felt (see page 100).

4. Add the embroidered embellishments and stitch the design following the pattern below.

5. Fold the doll so the curved edges line up behind the head. Sew across the top of the head using the Whip Stitch.

6. Use the Stab Stitch to sew up the back seam.

7. Stuff the doll firmly, then pin and sew the bottom circle in place using the Whip Stitch.

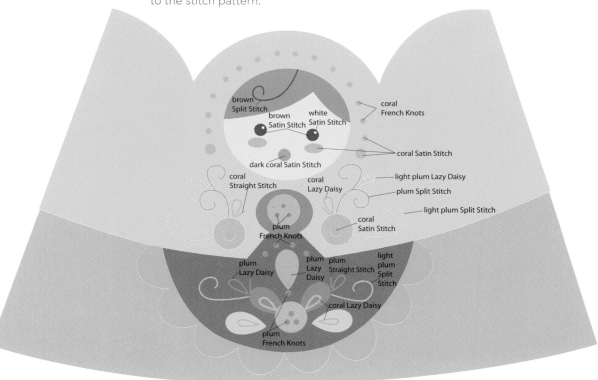

Enlarge 200%

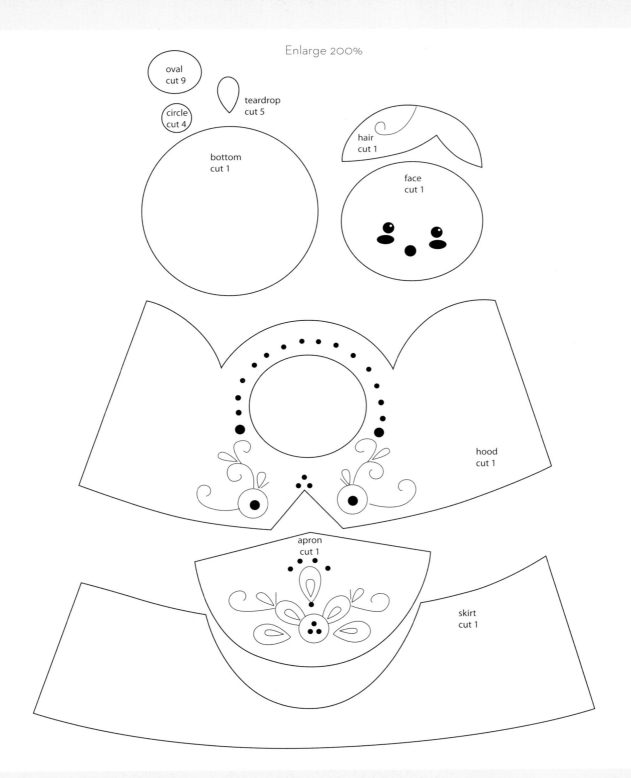

oval
cut 9

circle
cut 4

teardrop
cut 5

bottom
cut 1

hair
cut 1

face
cut 1

hood
cut 1

apron
cut 1

skirt
cut 1

Butterfly Wrist Cuff

× ×

This stitched cuff packs a punch of pretty color! The extra pop comes from a simple crayon tinting technique and sweet stitches in lots of colors.

WHAT YOU NEED

Template (page 43)

Piece of aqua quilter's cotton fabric, 10 x 6 inches (25.4 x 15.2 cm)

Wax crayons in pink, orange, and turquoise

White paper

Iron & ironing board

Embroidery floss, 1 skein each of orange, light orange, pink, turquoise, and aqua*

One ½-inch (1.3 cm) button

*The author used DMC embroidery floss colors 3853, 3854, 760, 597, and 598.

STITCHES

Blanket Stitch

Overcast Stitch

Satin Stitch

Stem Stitch

INSTRUCTIONS

1. Enlarge the template 125%.

2. Use the template to trace two wrist cuff shapes onto the fabric, allowing ½ inch (1.3 cm) of fabric around the edges. You can adjust the size as needed by measuring around your wrist and adding or subtracting half the needed measurement from each end. Keep in mind the ends will overlap 1½ inches (1.3 cm). Do not cut out the shapes yet.

3. Trace the butterfly design onto one of the fabric pieces.

4. Place the traced fabric onto a hard surface, and with the wax crayons, lightly begin filling in spaces on the pattern with color. Don't press too hard

Butterfly Wrist Cuff

and use very light strokes. You can go back and add more color if you want to, after step 5. Create blends by using more or darker strokes at the center points of each shape, lightening them as you go outward.

5. Place the colored fabric on a towel or ironing board, and place the paper on top of it. Using the hottest setting, press an iron over the paper. This will set the color into the fabric and remove any excess wax. Lift and press for a few minutes, until no more wax is being released onto the paper.

6. Embroider the butterfly design according to the pattern.

7. Cut out the two wrist cuffs ½ inch (1.3 cm) outside the template edge. Pin them together with right sides facing. Stitch them together around the edge, leaving one end open.

8. Trim off the stitched corners, clip the curved seam allowances, and turn the wrist cuff right side out. Push out the seams and press them flat.

9. Turn under the raw edges at the open end and sew it closed by hand.

10. Sew a Blanket Stitch with aqua floss all around the edge of the wrist cuff.

11. At one end, cut a ½-inch (1.3 cm) slit through both layers of fabric and use the Overcast Stitch around it to create a buttonhole. Sew the button on at the other end.

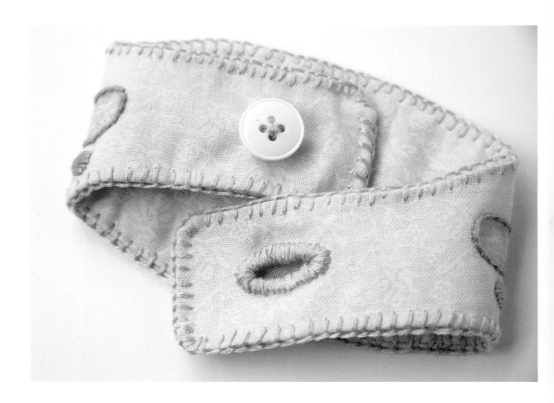

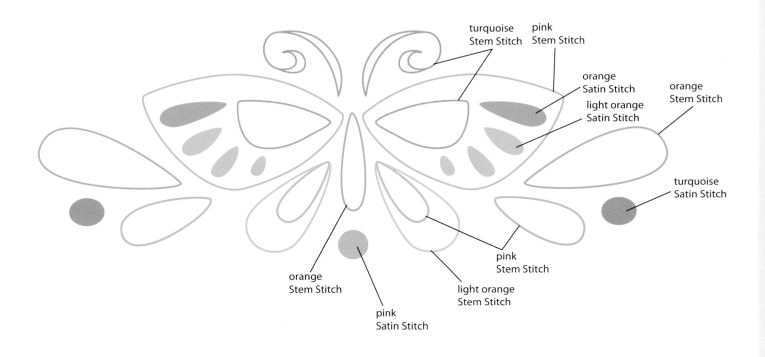

turquoise
Stem Stitch

pink
Stem Stitch

orange
Satin Stitch

light orange
Satin Stitch

orange
Stem Stitch

turquoise
Satin Stitch

orange
Stem Stitch

pink
Satin Stitch

pink
Stem Stitch

light orange
Stem Stitch

Enlarge 125%

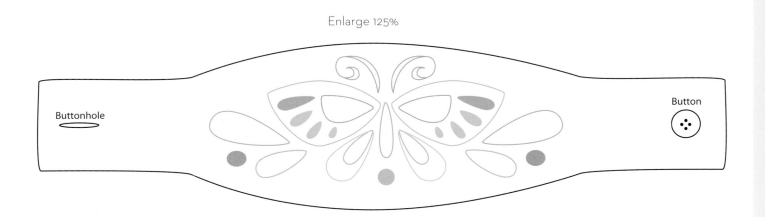

Buttonhole

Button

Owl Love Paper Card & Gift Tag

×××××××××××××××××××××××××××××××××××××××

Don't have time for a handmade gift? Make a card instead!
Simply add a bit of paint or colored pencil to this
sweet hand-stitched card and gift tag set.

WHAT YOU NEED

Cold press, heavyweight (140 lb) watercolor paper, or heavy card stock

Hole punch

Decorative scissors (optional)

Watercolor or acrylic paints and brushes, or colored pencils

Embroidery floss, 1 skein each of dark pink, pink, light pink, turquoise, aqua, and gray*

Scrap of pink satin ribbon, ½ inch (1.3 cm) wide

The author used DMC embroidery floss colors 3712, 760, 3713, 3810, 598, and 535.

STITCHES

Back Stitch

Lazy Daisy

Running Stitch

Satin Stitch

INSTRUCTIONS

1. For the card: cut a 6½ x 9-inch (16.5 x 22.9 cm) piece of watercolor paper. Lightly score it and fold it in half.

2. For the gift tag: cut a 2-inch (5.1 cm) circle and punch a hole in the top for the ribbon.

3. If you like, use decorative scissors to cut a fancy edge on the card and tag.

4. Trace the embroidery patterns onto the paper, using a light table or sunny window.

5. Get out your paints and fill in the designs with a bit of color. If you're using acrylics, use thin layers of paint; if you apply it too thickly, the paint may crack when you embroider over it. Allow the paint to dry.

6. Using 3 of the 6 threads of floss, begin stitching the designs. The Back Stitch is ideal for embroidering on paper. Just keep your stitches a little longer than usual so that the paper doesn't tear in between. If you have trouble getting the needle to come up in the right place from the underside of the paper, it helps a lot to punch needle holes through from the top first.

7. Cut a 6-inch (15.2 cm) piece of ribbon and tie it through the hole on the tag.

Variation

Maybe a stitched chipmunk is more your style? Grab the extra pattern on page 112.

Appliqué & Color   45

Canvas Cuckoo Clock

××××××××××××××××××××××××××××××××××××××

It's time to stitch up something fabulous! A bit of paint, creative embroidery,
and a working clock movement make this cuckoo clock unique.

WHAT YOU NEED

Template (page 49)

One stretched canvas, 9 x 12 inches
(22.9 x 30.5 cm)

Craft knife

Watercolor or acrylic paints
and brushes

Embroidery floss, 1 skein each of
turquoise, red brown, light brown,
brown, dark brown, green, light
green, and coral*

Staple gun

Clock kit with ¼-inch (0.6 cm) shaft
and hands that are 1 to 1½ inches
(2.5 to 3.8 cm) long

*The author used DMC embroidery floss
colors 598, 780, 437, 420, 433, 471, 472,
and 352.*

STITCHES

Back Stitch

Straight Stitch

French Knot

Satin Stitch

Scallop Stitch

Split Stitch

INSTRUCTIONS

1. Remove the canvas from the frame.
You can either remove the staples, or
you may need to cut the canvas off
with a craft knife. Just be sure to leave
enough canvas overlapping the back to
re-staple it later.

2. Enlarge the embroidery template
145% (or size to your liking), and trace
it onto the canvas using a light table or
sunny window.

3. Get out your paints and fill in the
designs with a bit of color. If you're using
acrylics, use thin layers of paint; if you
apply it too thickly, the paint may crack
when you embroider over it. Allow the
paint to dry thoroughly.

4. Begin stitching the design. Use all
6 threads for thicker lines, and 3 of the
6 threads of floss for thinner lines.

5. Put the finished canvas back onto the
frame and staple it in place.

6. Cut a hole in the center of the clock
face. Attach the clock parts according
to the instructions on the package.

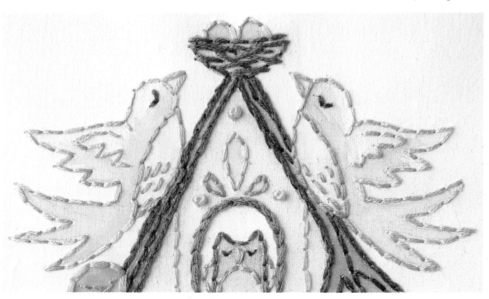

Canvas Cuckoo Clock

red brown
Back Stitch

turquoise
Back Stitch

light brown
Back Stitch

dark brown
Back Stitch

coral
Back Stitch

green
Back Stitch

light green
French Knot

coral
Straight Stitch

light green
Back Stitch

brown
Split Stitch

red brown
Back Stitch

light brown
Back Stitch

dark brown
Back Stitch

light brown
Back Stitch

green
Back Stitch

turquoise
Back Stitch

light brown
Split Stitch

light green
Satin Stitch

light green
Back Stitch

dark brown
Back Stitch

brown
Split Stitch

brown
Back Stitch

dark brown
Split Stitch

green
Back Stitch

red brown
Back Stitch

light green
Back Stitch

light brown
French Knot

red brown
Back Stitch

light brown
Satin Stitch

brown
Split Stitch

light brown
Back Stitch

light green
French Knot

green
Back Stitch

dark brown
Split Stitch

turquoise
Back Stitch

dark brown
Back Stitch

light brown
Back Stitch

green
Back Stitch

light green
Split Stitch

red brown
Back Stitch

light brown
Split Stitch

light brown
Scallop Stitch

light green
French Knot

green
Back Stitch

red brown
Back Stitch

light brown
Back Stitch

48

Enlarge 145%

Chapter 3

Redwork & Crewel

x x x x x x x x x x x x x x x x x x x x x x x x x x x x x x x x x x x x x x x x x x x x x x x x x x x

Redwork and Crewel are two forms of embroidery that stitchers have used decoratively for generations. Both are wonderful techniques you can use to make special, handmade gifts that will be treasured for years to come. Redwork is simple, easy for the beginner, and perfect for children's items such as the fun Storybook Panels on page 56. Crewel work is a bit more advanced. The patterns are very detailed and colorful, and make a great embellishment for a variety of household decorations.

Redwork

Redwork is embroidery stitched all in red on white fabric. It has been a popular form of stitching since the 19th century. Redwork patterns are stitched mostly with simple outline stitches and have traditionally been the samplers of choice for children learning embroidery. Redwork squares can often be seen on antique quilts. Many Redwork designs feature decorative florals or illustrate children and stories or nursery rhymes.

A Note about Needles

Crewel needles have extra large eyes that are easier to pass the thick wool thread through. If you have trouble threading your needle for Crewel work, try folding the end of the wool thread, pinching a crease and passing the bend through the needle.

Crewel

Crewel embroidery is stitched using thick, wool thread on linen fabric. The wool, along with the use of lots of dimensional stitches, creates a wonderful textured look that you just want to reach out and touch. Traditional Jacobean crewel designs feature lots of nature motifs. In the 1970s, crewel gained a new popularity that it still enjoys today. Traditional embroidery stitches are also used for crewel, but here are the special ones you'll need to know for the projects in this chapter.

Overcast Stitch

The Overcast Stitch is regularly used in crewel embroidery to create thick, raised lines. Begin by following the pattern line with a Split Stitch. Next, stitch the Overcast Stitch over the Split Stitch line. Start at A, slide the needle under the row of Split Stitches, not through the fabric. Bring the needle out at B. Repeat this stitch, covering the entire line.

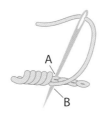

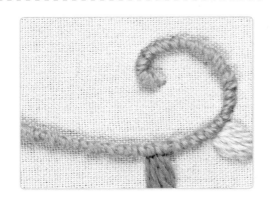

Trellis Couching Stitch

The Trellis Couching Stitch is almost exclusively used in crewel. Start by making several long Straight Stitches horizontally and vertically across the area. Space them ¼ to ⅛ inches (0.6 to 0.3 cm) apart. Next, make tiny stitches diagonally from A to B where the Straight Stitches cross to hold them in place, as in other types of couching.

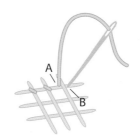

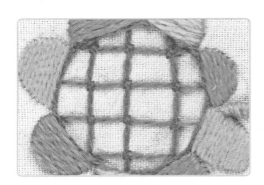

Snow White, Rose Red Fleece Scarf

× ×

For this cozy scarf, you'll stitch bright red snowflakes on white fleece. A clever technique using tissue paper makes it easy to embroider designs onto thick, soft fabrics.

WHAT YOU NEED

½ yard (0.5 m) of white fleece, 60 inches (152.4 cm) wide

Tissue paper

Embroidery floss, 1 skein of red*

The author used DMC embroidery floss color 321.

STITCHES

Back Stitch

French Knot

Hidden Stitch

Lazy Daisy

Satin Stitch

Straight Stitch

Topstitch

INSTRUCTIONS

1. Cut two strips of white fleece that measure 5½ x 60 inches (14 x 152.4 cm).

2. Transfer the snowflake designs onto tissue paper, using a light table or sunny window. Cut them out and arrange them at both ends of one strip of fleece. Pin the paper in place.

3. Embroider the designs through the tissue paper and fleece together, following the pattern lines. Use all 6 threads of floss for the larger snowflakes, and 3 threads for the smaller, thinner lines.

4. When you've finished stitching, carefully tear the tissue paper away from your stitches. A needle or tweezers will help remove small bits from under tight stitches.

5. Pin the two pieces of fleece together with right sides facing. Machine-stitch around the edges with a ½-inch (1.3 cm) seam allowance, leaving a 4-inch (10.2 cm) opening.

6. Trim the corners and snip off any excess fabric. Turn the scarf right side out through the opening. Push out the corners, and sew up the opening using the Hidden Stitch.

7. Press the seams flat and topstitch around the scarf ¼ inch (0.6 cm) from the edge.

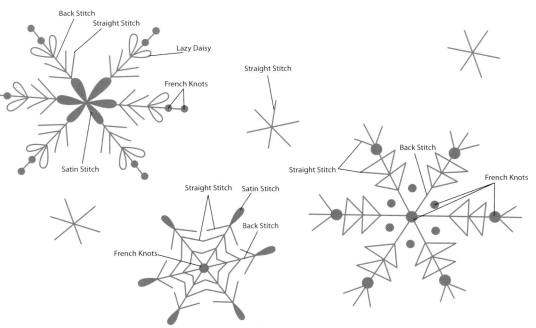

Hansel and Gretel Storybook Panels

Capture this beloved fairy tale with a set of embroidered panels. Although Redwork is traditionally stitched red on white, this pattern bends the rules just a bit to include pink as well.

WHAT YOU NEED

Templates (page 59)

4 pieces of white fabric,
14 x 15 inches (35.6 x 38.1 cm)

Embroidery floss, 2 skeins of red,
1 skein of pink*

8 wood canvas stretcher bars,
8 inches (20.3 cm) long

8 wood canvas stretcher bars,
9 inches (22.9 cm) long

4 pieces of white matte board,
8 x 9 inches (20.3 x 22.9 cm)

Staple gun

4 pieces of 1-inch-wide (2.5 cm) red
or pink ribbon, each 22 inches
(55.9 cm) long

*The author used DMC embroidery
floss colors 321 and 760.*

STITCHES

Lazy Daisy

Straight Stitch

Running Stitch

Satin Stitch

Split Stitch

INSTRUCTIONS

1. Enlarge the embroidery templates 220% (or size to your liking), and transfer them onto the fabric pieces.

2. Split your floss in half, using 3 of the 6 threads. Embroider the designs.

3. Fit pairs of stretcher bars together to form four 8 x 9-inch (20.3 x 22.9 cm) frames.

4. For each panel, place a piece of matte board over the frame and center an embroidery panel over it. Fold the edges of the panel tightly over the frame and matte board, and staple them in place on the back. (Start by placing one staple in each side, then fold the corners over, adding more staples as needed.) Trim off any extra fabric.

5. To make the hanger, tie a big bow in the center of each ribbon and staple the ends to each upper back corner of the panels.

Variation

Grab the extra Redwork sampler panel
on page 115.

Hansel and Gretel Storybook Panels

Enlarge 220%

Crewel Peacock Messenger Bag

×·×

Give your basic messenger bag a kitschy, retro feel with this cool crewel peacock pattern.

Variation

Try the extra peacock pattern (page 112) on for size.

WHAT YOU NEED

Template (at right)

Blue canvas bag (with a blank front flap to stitch on)

Fabric carbon paper

Crewel wool, 1 skein each of light green, green, light blue, blue, dark blue, aqua, and turquoise

Crewel needle

STITCHES

Overcast Stitch

Satin Stitch

Stem Stitch

Straight Stitch

INSTRUCTIONS

1. Enlarge the embroidery template 150% (or size to your liking) and transfer it to the bag flap using the carbon paper.

2. Embroider the design according to the pattern.

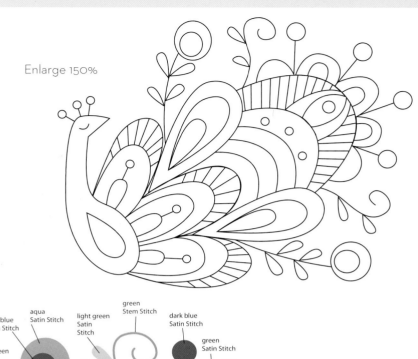

Enlarge 150%

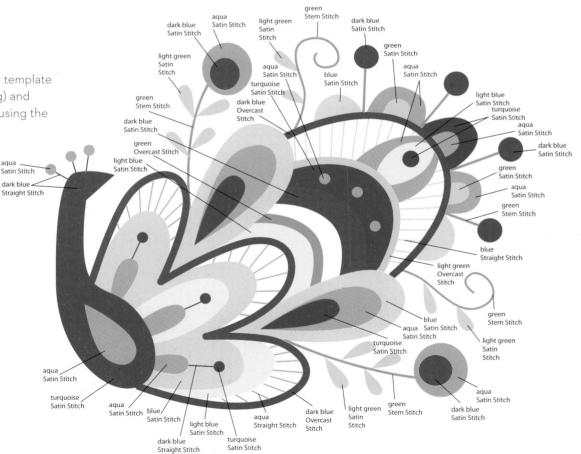

Crewel Family Tree

× ×

Tell your family story in crewel. This lovely tree has spots
for many names and new additions!

WHAT YOU NEED

Template (page 65)

½ yard (0.5 m) of white linen

Crewel wool, 1 skein each of light
green, green, dark green, light
coral, coral, dark coral, yellow,
purple, light brown, brown, and
dark brown

Crewel needle

*The author used DMC embroidery
floss colors 3712, 760, 3713, 3810, 598,
and 535.*

STITCHES

Back Stitch

French Knot

Overcast Stitch

Running Stitch

Satin Stitch

Stem Stitch

Straight Stitch

Trellis Couching Stitch

INSTRUCTIONS

1. Cut a 15 x 17-inch (38.1 x 43.2 cm)
piece of linen. Enlarge the embroidery
template 170% (or size to your liking),
and transfer it onto the fabric.

2. Embroider the design according to
the pattern.

3. When you've finished, turn under
the edges 1 inch (2.5 cm) and hem with
a Running Stitch ½ inch (1.3 cm) from
the edge.

4. Draw or trace two 1¼-inch (3.2 cm)
circles on the linen for each name you
want on your tree, leaving at least
1 inch (2.5 cm) of space between the
circles. (Each name circle will have an
embroidered front and a blank back that
will be stitched together.) For longer
names, you can make ovals. Do not cut
out the circles yet.

5. Write the names on the circles and
embroider them using the Back Stitch.
Sew a Running Stitch around the edge
of each circle, stitching directly on the
drawn pencil line.

6. Add a ½-inch (1.3 cm) margin around
each circle, then cut them out. With
right sides facing, pin each front name
circle to a blank back. Stitch the circles

together using a ¼-inch (0.6 cm) seam
allowance and leaving a ½-inch (1.3 cm)
opening for turning.

7. Turn each circle right side out, press
flat, and sew up the opening. Sew each
name onto the tree panel.

8. Frame your keepsake crewel art!

Crewel Family Tree

yellow
Overcast Stitch

coral
Satin Stitch

coral
Stem Stitch

light coral
Satin Stitch

dark coral
French Knots

green
Stem Stitch

dark brown
Satin Stitch

light brown
Satin Stitch

green
Stem Stitch

green
Satin Stitch

dark green
Overcast Stitch

brown
Straight Stitch

light green
Satin Stitch

light green
Stem Stitch

light coral
Straight Stitch

light coral
Overcast Stitch

coral
Satin Stitch

coral
Trellis
Couching

purple
Satin Stitch

light green
Satin Stitch

light green
Stem Stitch

green
Overcast Stitch

coral
Satin Stitch

light brown
Stem Stitch

dark green
Stem Stitch

dark green
Overcast Stitch

light coral
Satin Stitch

dark green
Stem Stitch

yellow
Satin Stitch

yellow
Satin Stitch

dark green
Straight Stitch

green
Overcast Stitch

coral
Satin Stitch

light coral
Satin Stitch

light coral
Satin Stitch

dark green
Stem Stitch

dark brown
Satin Stitch

brown
Overcast Stitch

dark brown
Stem Stitch

brown
Stem Stitch

brown
Straight Stitch

light brown
Stem Stitch

light brown
Straight Stitch

light coral
Satin Stitch

dark coral
French Knots

light green
Satin Stitch

light green
Stem Stitch

light green
Stem Stitch

dark coral
Stem Stitch

coral
Satin Stitch

brown
Stem Stitch

yellow
Satin Stitch

light green
Stem Stitch

light green
Satin Stitch

green
Stem Stitch

green
Satin Stitch

dark green
Stem Stitch

dark green
Overcast Stitch

coral
Stem Stitch

purple
Satin Stitch

dark coral
Overcast Stitch

coral
Straight Stitch

yellow
Satin Stitch

coral
Satin Stitch

green
Satin Stitch

dark green
Overcast Stitch

green
Satin Stitch

light green
Overcast Stitch

yellow
Satin Stitch

purple
Satin Stitch

yellow
French Knots

dark coral
Satin Stitch

coral
Satin Stitch

green
Stem Stitch

green
Satin Stitch

Enlarge 170%

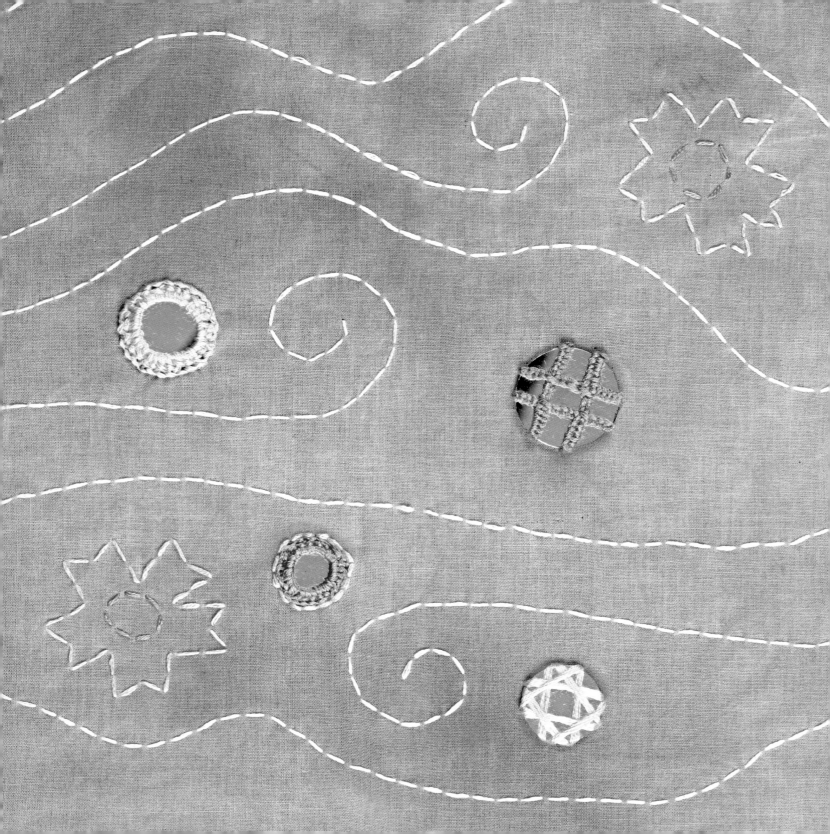

Chapter 4

Sashiko & Shisha

x x x x x x x x x x x x x x x x x x x x x x x x x x x x x x x x x x x x x x x x x x x

Sashiko and Shisha have both been around since ancient times and are still used today to enhance fabrics in beautiful ways. Sashiko patterns are simple and repetitive but produce wonderful results perfect for linens or other household items like the curtains and placemats in this chapter. Shisha embroidery is a unique way to add sparkle, shine, and other dimensional elements to your work.

Sashiko

Sashiko is an ancient form of embroidery from Japan. Traditionally, it was used as a functional form of stitching to repair tears or worn spots on fabric. Now it is often used for decoration and consists of beautiful designs—sometimes simple, sometimes complex, but usually geometric—stitched entirely in white thread on indigo fabric.

A Note about Needles

You will want to use specific types of needles when stitching Sashiko and Crewel embroidery. Sashiko needles are longer and thinner than regular embroidery needles to allow you to make several running stitches at once.

Sashiko Stitch

Sashiko designs are usually stitched with the Running Stitch and without the use of a hoop. Use an extra long needle so you can create several stitches at once on the loose fabric. This technique works best on designs with straight lines. If you find it easier, you can make stitches one at a time and achieve the same results.

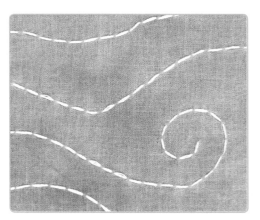

Shisha

Shisha embroidery originated in ancient Persia and is now most popular in India where it is used in colorful, intricate designs decorating clothing and wall hangings. The Shisha Stitch is used to attach tiny mirrors to fabric, but can also be used to attach anything flat. Try using the Shisha Stitch to attach coins, bottle caps, large sequins, guitar picks, shells, flat stones, or anything else you can think of to your embroidery projects.

Shisha Stitch

To attach a mirror to fabric using the Shisha Stitch, first stitch four Straight Stitches across the mirror vertically and horizontally to hold it in place. Next, stitch four more Straight Stitches across diagonally to form a star shape. Keep these stitches tight and not too close to the edge of the mirror.

Now bring the needle and floss up at A and under the Straight Stitches from the center at B. Pass the tip of the needle over the floss, making a Blanket Stitch.

Repeat this step, then make another tiny stitch along the outside edge, catching the previous stitch and a tiny bit of fabric at C. Pass the needle over the floss again, and pull it tight to the fabric. Repeat this stitch all the way around the mirror.

When you've attached the mirror, you can embroider pretty borders around the edge. Try using the Split Stitch or Chain Stitch.

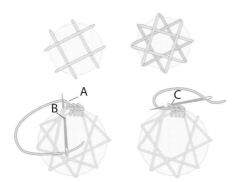

Buttonhole Connectors

Buttonhole Connectors can also be used to attach mirrors or other objects to embroidery. To create a Buttonhole Connector, make four Straight Stitches vertically and horizontally across the mirror. Make a loose, diagonal stitch over the Straight Stitch from A to B. Bring the needle up again at C, catching the floss under the needle and pulling it tight over the Straight Stitch. Work a row of Buttonhole Stitches over each Straight Stitch, forming thick cords to hold the mirror in place.

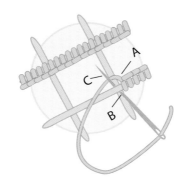

Pond and Scales Sashiko Placemats

x x x x x x x x x x x x x x x x x x x x x x x x x x x x x x x x x x x x x x x x x x x x

Infuse plain placemats with a striking stitched pattern! Placemats are the perfect canvas for practice with Sashiko ... and you can enjoy your handiwork with every meal.

WHAT YOU NEED

Pattern (page 72)

1 yard (0.9 m) of dark blue quilter's cotton fabric

Carbon transfer paper

Embroidery floss, 1 skein each of white, light pink, and pink*

Dark blue thread

The author used DMC embroidery floss colors white, 761, and 760.

Note: The instructions are for two 16 x 12-inch (40.6 x 30.5 cm) placemats.

STITCHES

Running Stitch

Topstitch

INSTRUCTIONS

1. For each placemat, cut two pieces of 17 x 13-inch (43.2 x 33 cm) rectangles from the fabric.

2. Enlarge one of the Sashiko patterns 200% (or size to your liking).

3. Transfer the Sashiko pattern to a piece of fabric, using a light color of transfer paper.

4. Embroider the design. Sashiko designs are usually stitched with an extra long needle, so you can create several stitches at once. But you can stitch them one at a time if you prefer and achieve the same results.

5. Pin two pieces of fabric together with right sides facing and stitch 1 inch (2.5 cm) from the edge, leaving a 2-inch (5.1 cm) opening. Trim off the corners and turn the placemat right side out through the opening. Push out the corners and press the seams flat.

6. Topstitch the placemat 1/8 inch (0.3 cm) from the edge on all sides.

7. Repeat the process for the second placement, using the other Sashiko design.

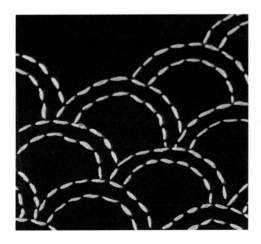

Pond and Scales Sashiko Placemats

Enlarge 200%

Variation

Use the extra Sashiko pattern on page 116 on your placemats instead or try it on the edge of a skirt for a pretty stitched border.

Sashiko Café Curtain

××

Using some variations from traditional Sashiko, this curtain
incorporates a lighter fabric and a bit of colored thread, giving
this repeating pattern a bit of added interest.

Sashiko Café Curtain

WHAT YOU NEED

Template (below)

1 yard (0.9 m) or more of blue quilter's cotton fabric

Fabric carbon paper

Blue thread to match the fabric

Embroidery floss, 1 skein each of blue and dark blue*

The author used DMC embroidery floss colors 793 and 792.

STITCHES

Running Stitch

INSTRUCTIONS

1. Measure your window to determine how large to make your curtain panels. For a single panel, a general rule is to use fabric that is 1½ times the width of your window. Add an extra 3 inches (7.6 cm) to the length.

2. Hem the sides and bottom of your curtain with a double-fold hem to hide any raw edges. Fold under the top edge ½ inch (1.3 cm), then another 2 inches (5.1 cm) and press. Stitch along the fold to create a casing for the curtain rod.

3. Enlarge the embroidery template 125% (or size to your liking) and transfer it to the bottom of the curtain, repeating it all along the edge.

4. Embroider the design. Sashiko designs are usually stitched without a hoop using an extra long needle, so you can create several stitches at once on the loose fabric. If you find it easier, you can make stitches one at a time and achieve the same results.

Enlarge 125%

Shisha Skirt

× ×

Update a plain, khaki skirt with subtle sparkle. Shisha mirrors become little "buds" on a beautiful stitched branch.

Shisha Skirt

WHAT YOU NEED

Tan twill/denim skirt

Carbon transfer paper

Embroidery floss, 1 skein each of coral, light coral, and brown*

Two 1-inch (2.5 cm) round Shisha mirrors

Three ¾-inch (1.9 cm) round Shisha mirrors

The author used DMC embroidery floss colors 352, 353, and 420.

STITCHES

Satin Stitch

Shisha Stitch

Stem Stitch

INSTRUCTIONS

1. Transfer the embroidery pattern onto the bottom corner of the skirt, using transfer paper.

2. Embroider the designs, beginning with the branch.

3. Position the mirrors and stitch them in place one by one.

Variation

Want a different look? Try the extra pattern on page 114 on your skirt, your shirt sleeve, or anywhere you like.

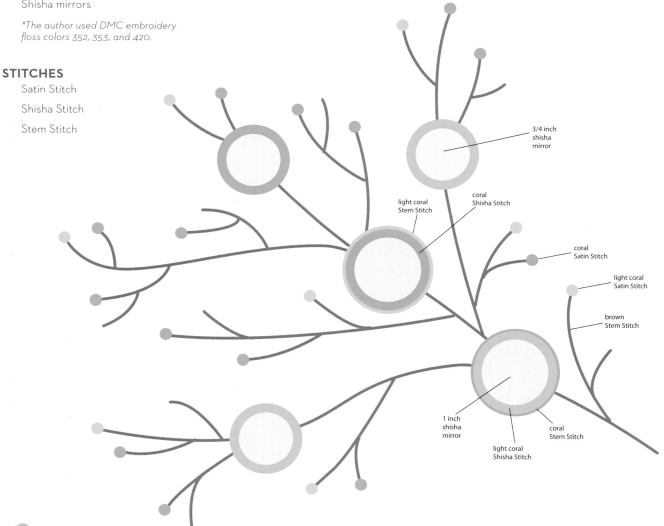

3/4 inch shisha mirror

light coral Stem Stitch

coral Shisha Stitch

coral Satin Stitch

light coral Satin Stitch

brown Stem Stitch

1 inch shisha mirror

light coral Shisha Stitch

coral Stem Stitch

Nature Walk Banner

× ×

Capture a bit of natural inspiration using Shisha embroidery techniques.
Shells, feathers, and stones find a lovely home on this stitched banner.

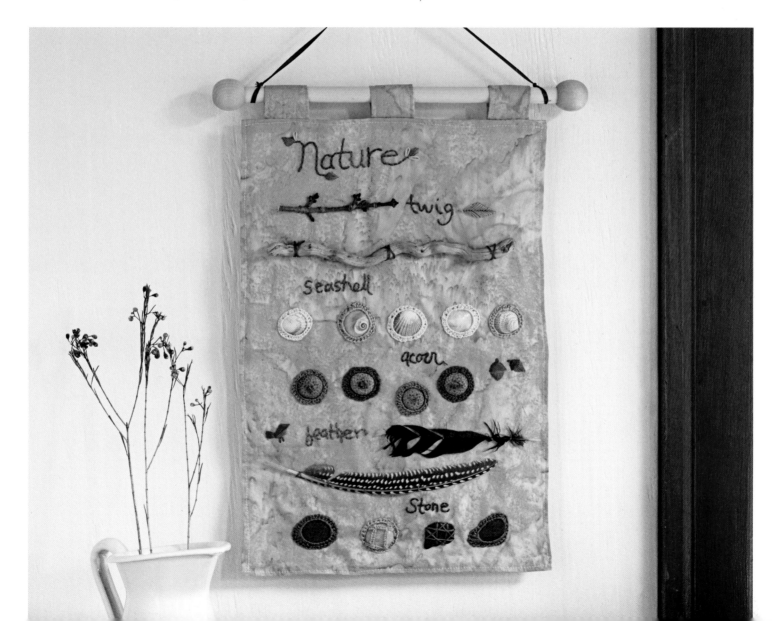

Nature Walk Banner

WHAT YOU NEED

Templates (page 79)

1 piece of green quilter's cotton fabric, 10 x 15 inches (25.4 x 38.1 cm) or big enough to hold your nature items

3 pieces of matching fabric, 2 x 4 inches (5.1 x 10.2 cm)

Nature items: flat stones, acorn tops, seashells, twigs, feathers, and so forth

Embroidery floss, various browns and greens of your choice*

1½-inch-wide (3.8 cm) dowel rod, at least 2 inches (5.1 cm) longer than the finished width of your panel

2 wooden dowel caps, 1-inch (2.5 cm) round with ½-inch (1.3 cm) holes

White glue

15-inch (38.1 cm) piece of narrow, brown ribbon

The author used DMC embroidery floss colors 470, 471, 472, 975, 433, 869, 420, 829, 611, 422, and 712.

STITCHES

Back Stitch

Buttonhole Connector Stitch

Lazy Daisy

Satin Stitch

Shisha Stitch

INSTRUCTIONS

1. Make a double-fold hem on the sides and bottom edge of the fabric panel. Also make a narrow double-fold hem on the long sides of each small strip of fabric.

2. Fold the top edge of the panel toward the wrong side. Fold the strips in half and pin them along the top with raw edges behind the panel, one at each end and one in the center. Stitch across the top edge, catching the ends of the strips in the stitching.

3. Lay out the fabric panel and arrange your nature collection on it. Decide where you want to embroider the words and elements. It's a good idea to keep heavier items, such as stones, near the bottom; they will help hold your panel straight. You can make small marks on the fabric so you remember where each piece goes, or take a photograph to refer to later.

4. Enlarge the embroidery templates 175% (or size to your liking) and transfer them to the fabric, or write any words you want in your own handwriting. Embroider the designs.

5. Now begin attaching the nature items to the panel. Start with flat items like stones or shells, attaching them with the Shisha Stitch. For more rounded stones, shells, or acorn tops, try using only the first part of the Shisha Stitch (stop at the star) or create four

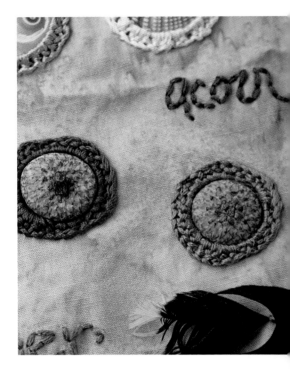

Buttonhole Connectors over the piece to hold it in place. You can embroider pretty borders around the edge after it's stitched on.

6. Now sew twigs or feathers in place with small stitches over them every couple of inches.

7. Slide the dowel into the fabric loops at the top of the panel and glue a dowel cap over each end.

8. Tie one end of the ribbon at both ends of the dowel so you can hang your banner.

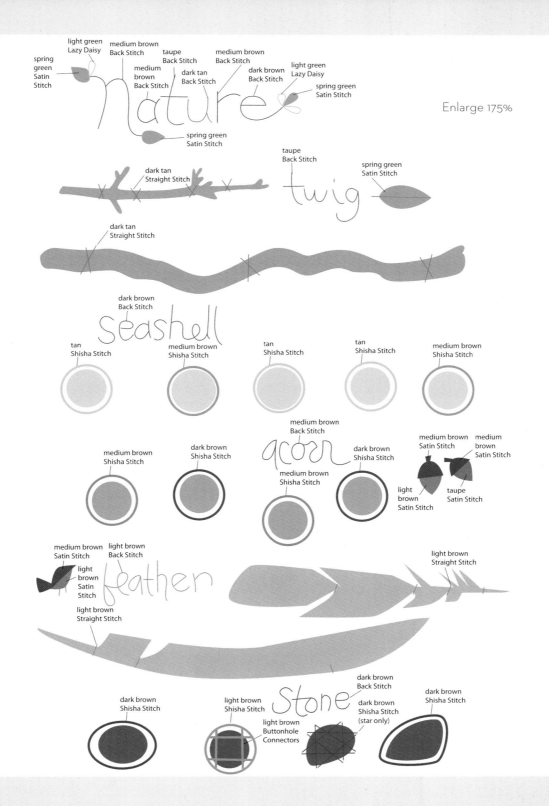

light green
Lazy Daisy

spring
green
Satin
Stitch

medium brown
Back Stitch

medium
brown
Back Stitch

taupe
Back Stitch

dark tan
Back Stitch

medium brown
Back Stitch

dark brown
Back Stitch

light green
Lazy Daisy

spring green
Satin Stitch

spring green
Satin Stitch

nature

Enlarge 175%

dark tan
Straight Stitch

taupe
Back Stitch

spring green
Satin Stitch

twig

dark tan
Straight Stitch

dark brown
Back Stitch

seashell

tan
Shisha Stitch

medium brown
Shisha Stitch

tan
Shisha Stitch

tan
Shisha Stitch

medium brown
Shisha Stitch

medium brown
Shisha Stitch

dark brown
Shisha Stitch

medium brown
Back Stitch

dark brown
Shisha Stitch

medium brown
Satin Stitch

medium
brown
Satin Stitch

acorn

medium brown
Shisha Stitch

light
brown
Satin
Stitch

taupe
Satin Stitch

medium brown
Satin Stitch

light brown
Back Stitch

light
brown
Satin
Stitch

light brown
Straight Stitch

feather

light brown
Straight Stitch

dark brown
Back Stitch

dark brown
Shisha Stitch

stone

dark brown
Shisha Stitch

light brown
Shisha Stitch

light brown
Buttonhole
Connectors

dark brown
Shisha Stitch
(star only)

dark brown
Shisha Stitch

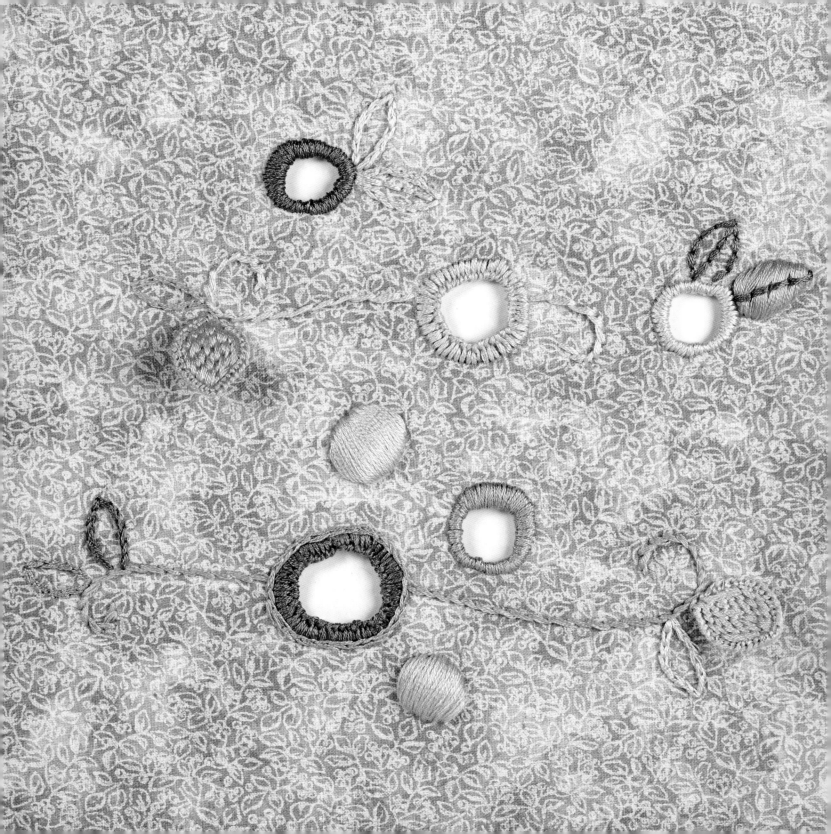

Chapter 5

Cutwork & Stumpwork

× ×

Cutwork and Stumpwork are unique ways to add dimension to
your embroidery. In Cutwork, windows are cut into the fabric
and reinforced with special embroidered stitches. This technique
is particularly striking when a different color of fabric is placed
behind the cutwork piece, as in the Fancy Feather Throw Pillow. In
Stumpwork, three-dimensional shapes are created and attached to the
background fabric. Since Stumpwork is raised and can be delicate,
it is best used for art pieces or other items that
won't get a lot of wear and tear.

Cutwork

There are two stitches used to create Cutwork holes: the Buttonhole and the Overcast Stitch. I've found that the Buttonhole Stitch can be worked before cutting the fabric, while the Overcast Stitch works best after you've cut the hole.

Buttonhole Stitch

The Buttonhole Stitch is worked the same way as the Blanket Stitch, only the stitches are smaller and very close together. Trace the shape you want to cut out onto the fabric. Stitch a Buttonhole outline around the window shape, keeping the knotted edge of the stitch facing the section that will be cut out. Make a loose, diagonal stitch from A to B. Bring the needle up again at C, catching the floss under the needle and pulling it tight to the fabric. Repeat this stitch all around the window line. Next, cut the fabric away at the center and pull the leftover edges around to the back

of your stitches where it will be hidden. Then carefully trim the edges off as closely as you can to the row of stitches.

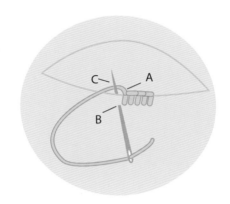

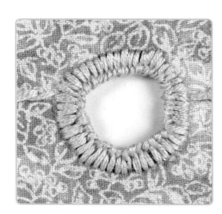

Overcast Stitch

The Overcast Stitch is similar to the Whip Stitch, except that Overcast Stitches are smaller and closer together, completely covering the raw edge of the fabric. First stitch a row of Running Stitches around the cutting pattern and then cut out the center piece of fabric. The hole will usually end up larger than the space you cut, so keep your cutting ⅛ inch (0.3 cm) inside the pattern line. Starting at the back of the fabric, bring your needle and floss through at A. Bring the needle over the edge of the

fabric and reinsert it from the back at B. Repeat all around the hole.

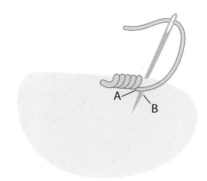

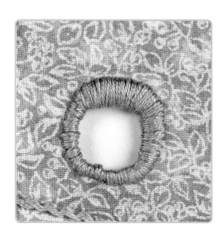

Stumpwork

Stumpwork is used to create three-dimensional embroidery art. There are several techniques specific to this style, but I have some favorites. One technique is to stuff a small piece of felt and stitch over it with a Satin Stitch, creating slight dimension. A second technique is to create a flat shape using fabric and wire and attach it to the background at one edge so that it will stand up.

Padded Stumpwork

To create a padded Stumpwork shape, start by stitching a felt piece in place onto the background using the Stab or Whip Stitch, tucking a small amount of stuffing underneath. Keep your stitches small and close together. Using the Satin Stitch, stitch horizontally over each felt piece to create a raised pillow shape.

Wired Stumpwork

This technique is a great way to make wings, flower petals, leaves, or anything with dimension. To create a wired Stumpwork piece, first bend a small piece of thin wire into the right size and shape. Leave ½-inch (1.3 cm) tails of wire at the bottom. Place the wire flatly onto another piece of fabric and stitch tiny stitches over the wire to secure it in place. Fill the wire shape with Long and Short Stitches. Stitch a Buttonhole Stitch tightly over the wire, with the knotted edge toward the outside. Leave the remaining floss attached when you finish.

Cut the shape out of the fabric. Carefully cut the excess fabric off as closely as you can to the Buttonhole Stitch. Poke the ends of the wire through the fabric and twist them together at the back. Bend them against the back of the fabric, cut them shorter if needed, and stitch them in place. Use the remaining floss from the shape to stitch the bottom edge in place on your work.

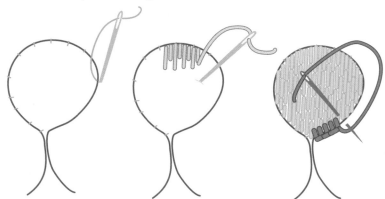

Hanging Lanterns Stumpwork

× ×

Create embroidered art with dimension. A crane and
a pair of lanterns almost pop off the fabric.

WHAT YOU NEED

Templates (page 86)

Piece of white cotton fabric, 6 x 6 inches
(15.2 x 15.2 cm)

4-inch (10.2 cm) wooden
embroidery hoop

Embroidery floss, 1 skein each of plum,
light plum, pink, dark pink, orange,
dark orange, dark plum, brown, and
light pink*

Small scraps of pink, orange, and
purple felt

Stuffing

Thin wire

White craft glue

3 yards (2.7 m) of satin ribbon, ½ inch
(1.3 cm) wide

*The author used DMC embroidery floss
colors 3835, 3836, 3713, 3712, 3854, 922, 3834,
420, and 760.*

STITCHES

Back Stitch

Buttonhole Stitch

Lazy Daisy

Long and Short Stitch

Satin Stitch

Stem Stitch

Straight Stitch

INSTRUCTIONS

1. Center and transfer the pattern onto
the fabric, and stretch the fabric onto
the hoop.

2. Begin by embroidering the branch
and flowers.

3. Using the templates, cut the two
lantern shapes and one crane wing
from felt.

4. Position the two lantern shapes on
the background. Sew the pieces in
place, using the Stab or Whip Stitch,
and tucking a small amount of stuffing
underneath as you work. Keep your
stitches small and close together.

5. Using the Satin Stitch, sew
horizontally over each felt piece to
create two padded stumpwork shapes.

Hanging Lanterns Stumpwork

6. With the darker matching floss, sew a few Straight Stitch lines horizontally over the top of each lantern shape. Don't pull your stitches too tightly.

7. For the crane, sew the felt wing in place, but without stuffing it. Continue with the Satin Stitch, vertically this time.

8. Embroider the remaining background details of the crane and lanterns.

9. To make the front crane wire stumpwork wing, bend a small piece of wire into the right size and shape. Leave ½-inch (1.3 cm) tails of wire at the bottom. Place the wire flatly onto a piece of cotton fabric and make tiny stitches over the wire to secure it in place.

10. Fill the wire shape with Long and Short Stitches. Sew a Buttonhole Stitch tightly over the wire, with the knotted edge towards the outside. Leave the remaining floss attached when you finish.

11. Cut the wing shape out of the fabric. Carefully cut the excess fabric off as closely as you can to the Buttonhole Stitch.

12. Poke the ends of the wire through the fabric at the bottom of the embroidered crane shape and twist them together behind the fabric. Bend the ends up over the floss behind the crane and sew them down. Use the remaining floss from the wing to sew the bottom edge in place to the bottom of the crane.

13. Trim off the fabric around the edge of the hoop to ½ inch (1.3 cm). Spread white glue along the inside of the inner hoop and fold the fabric over it, pressing it down. Allow the glue to dry with the hoop in place.

14. Remove the outer hoop and begin wrapping it with ribbon, gluing the ribbon down as you go around.

15. Replace the outer hoop, and hang your creation on the wall.

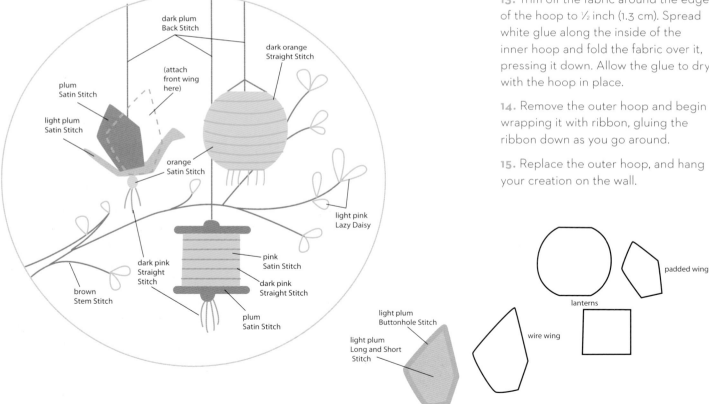

dark plum
Back Stitch

dark orange
Straight Stitch

(attach front wing here)

plum
Satin Stitch

light plum
Satin Stitch

orange
Satin Stitch

light pink
Lazy Daisy

brown
Stem Stitch

dark pink
Straight Stitch

pink
Satin Stitch

dark pink
Straight Stitch

plum
Satin Stitch

light plum
Buttonhole Stitch

light plum
Long and Short
Stitch

wire wing

lanterns

padded wing

Merry Mushroom Pincushion

Mushrooms made even cuter? You'll want to sew all day
using this cute, stumpwork pincushion at your side.

Merry Mushroom Pincushion

WHAT YOU NEED

Templates (page 89)

2 pieces of felt, green and blue, at least 7 inches (17.8 cm) square

Small scraps of red and white felt

Embroidery floss, 1 skein each of dark coral, coral, light coral, green, and white*

Stuffing

*The author used DMC embroidery floss colors 349, 351, 352, 471, and white.

STITCHES

Running Stitch

Satin Stitch

Stab Stitch

Straight Stitch

Whip Stitch

Variation

Stitch a lovely field of flowers and a sweet bunny on your pincushion instead: see the extra pattern on page 117.

INSTRUCTIONS

1. Transfer the templates onto the felt and cut out the pincushion side, the grass strip, and the mushroom shapes (five tops and five bottoms). Also cut two 2-inch (5.1 cm) circles for the top and base: one green, one blue.

2. Sew the green strip to the blue felt using small Running Stitches.

3. Position the white mushroom bottoms on the felt background, spacing them evenly around the pincushion and leaving room above each one for the mushroom tops. You can flip some over to the "wrong" side for variety. Sew them on using the Stab Stitch, keeping your stitches small and close together.

4. Using white floss, sew Satin Stitches vertically over each white felt piece.

5. Sew each mushroom top in place, tucking a small amount of stuffing underneath. Sew a horizontal Satin Stitch over each felt piece.

6. Sew a few white Satin Stitch spots on each mushroom top. Don't pull your stitches too tightly.

7. Sew a few blades of grass using the Straight Stitch.

8. Fold the embroidered felt strip into a circle, overlapping the ends slightly. Sew the ends together using the Whip Stitch.

9. Sew the bottom circle in place at the base with a Whip Stitch.

10. Sew the top circle in place at the top with a Whip Stitch, tucking stuffing inside before closing the seam.

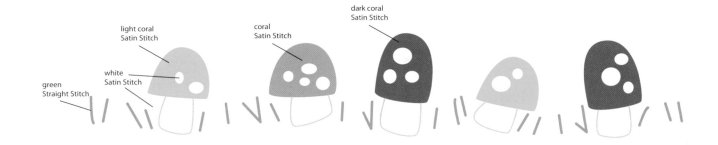

green Straight Stitch

white Satin Stitch

light coral Satin Stitch

coral Satin Stitch

dark coral Satin Stitch

pincushion side

grass strip

mushroom tops and stems

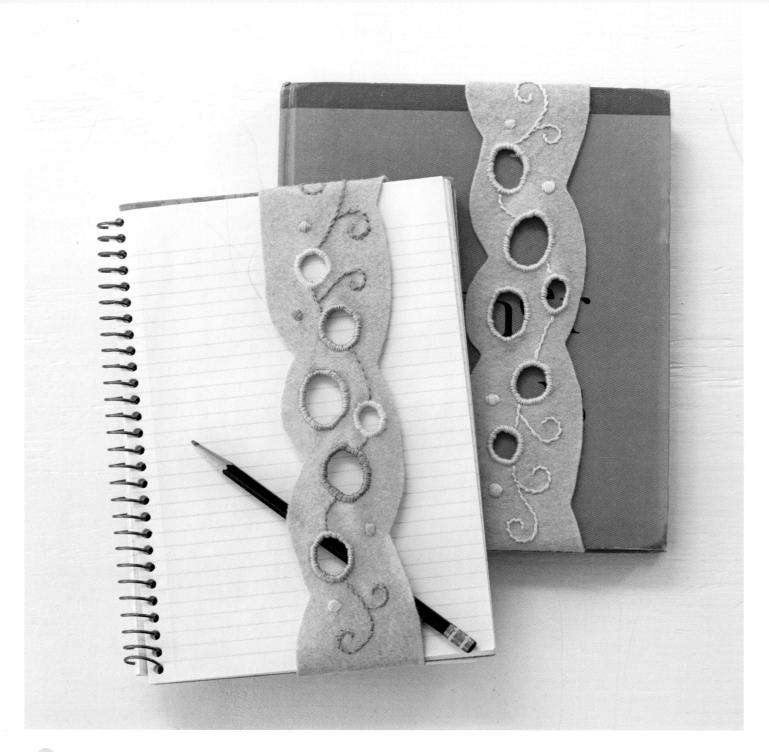

Cutwork Felt Bookmark

× ×

Save your place in style. This bookmark is adjustable to fit books from about 7 to 10 inches (17.8 to 25.4 cm) tall. However, you can alter the pattern to fit any sized book.

WHAT YOU NEED

Template (page 92)

1 piece of green or orange felt, 2½ x 12 inches (6.4 x 30.5 cm)

2 pieces of green or orange felt, 2½ x 5 inches (6.4 x 12.7 cm)

Embroidery floss, 1 skein of light green; or 1 skein each of aqua, orange, and yellow*

2 pieces of hook-and-loop tape, 3 inches (7.6 cm) long

*The author used DMC embroidery floss colors 772, 3817, 3853, and 3855.

STITCHES

Cross Stitch

Overcast Stitch

Satin Stitch

Stem Stitch

INSTRUCTIONS

1. Enlarge the bookmark template 160% (or size to your liking), transfer it onto the large piece of felt, and cut it out.

2. Sew the Overcast Stitch around the holes, then finish the design with the Stem and Satin Stitches.

3. Use a Cross Stitch to sew the short pieces of felt to both ends of the long piece, overlapping the pieces by ¼ inch (0.6 cm).

4. Sew two rows of hook-and-loop tape to both ends of the bookmark. Wrap the bookmark around your favorite book and secure the hook-and-loop tape in the back.

Cutwork Felt Bookmark

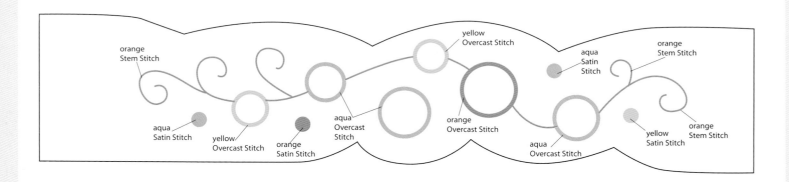

orange
Stem Stitch

yellow
Overcast Stitch

aqua
Satin
Stitch

orange
Stem Stitch

aqua
Satin Stitch

yellow
Overcast Stitch

orange
Satin Stitch

aqua
Overcast
Stitch

orange
Overcast Stitch

aqua
Overcast Stitch

yellow
Satin Stitch

orange
Stem Stitch

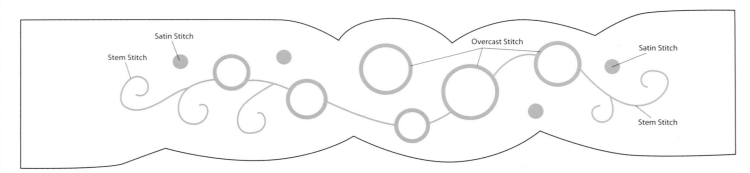

Satin Stitch

Stem Stitch

Overcast Stitch

Satin Stitch

Stem Stitch

Enlarge 160%

Fancy Feathers Throw Pillow

××××××××××××××××××××××××××××××××

The cutwork technique creates a neat peek-a-boo effect
on this soft and sweet accent pillow.

Fancy Feathers Throw Pillow

WHAT YOU NEED

Template (page 95)

2 pieces of lavender cotton fabric, 11 x 11 inches (27.9 x 27.9 cm)

Embroidery floss, 1 skein each of dark plum, plum, light plum, blue, light blue, aqua, and turquoise*

Fabric scraps, aqua or another contrasting color

Stuffing

*The author used DMC embroidery floss colors 3834, 3835, 3836, 3807, 341, 598, and 3810.

STITCHES

Back Stitch

Stem Stitch

Buttonhole Stitch

Overcast Stitch

Satin Stitch

INSTRUCTIONS

1. Transfer the feather template onto one of the lavender fabric squares.

2. Begin by stitching the center lines of the feathers in the Buttonhole Stitch. Keep the knotted edge of the stitch facing where the cutaway sections will be.

3. Cut away the fabric in the hole area, ⅛ inch (0.3 cm) inside the pattern line. Now finish the edge of the hole with the Overcast Stitch.

4. Continue embroidering the rest of the design according to the pattern. Edging the feathers with Back Stitching will keep your cutwork holes tight and neat looking.

5. When you're finished embroidering, pin the contrasting fabric piece to the back of your embroidered piece. Using tiny stitches in one thread of floss that matches the embroidery, stitch the top piece to the bottom around the cutwork holes.

6. Pin the pillow front to the back, right sides facing. Stitch around the edge, leaving a 3-inch (7.6 cm) opening on one side. Trim the corners.

7. Turn the pillow right side out and push out the corners. Stuff firmly and sew the hole closed.

turquoise
Buttonhole Stitch

cut out hole

purple
Back Stitch

blue
Satin Stitch

light blue
Back Stitch

plum
Satin Stitch

turquoise
Back Stitch

light plum
Satin Stitch

dark plum
Back Stitch

plum
Back Stitch

light blue
Satin Stitch

light plum
Satin Stitch

aqua
Satin Stitch

cut out
hole

plum
Satin Stitch

plum
Overcast
Stitch

blue
Buttonhole Stitch

light plum
Back Stitch

aqua
Satin Stitch

light plum
Buttonhole
Stitch

turquoise
Buttonhole Stitch

plum
Overcast Stitch

turquoise
Overcast Stitch

cut out hole

cut out
hole

aqua
Back Stitch

turquoise
Overcast Stitch

plum
Satin Stitch

aqua
Satin Stitch

cut out
hole

light blue
Satin Stitch

dark plum
Satin Stitch

blue
Satin Stitch

plum
Back Stitch

plum
Stem Stitch

dark plum
Stem Stitch

blue
Stem Stitch

turquoise
Stem Stitch

Variation

Trade feathers in for flowers with the
extra pattern on page 114.

Stitch Basics

You may already know the basics of embroidery and be ready to dive into the projects in this book. But if you've never embroidered before, you'll want to read through this section to get familiar with the tools of the trade and how to use them.

Basic Materials & Tools

Basic embroidery requires only a few inexpensive tools and materials that you can find at any craft store or even in your own stash of craft supplies. All you really need to get started is a needle, floss, hoop, and some fabric, but there are a few other items that will come in handy as well.

Floss

You can embroider with just about any thread or string, but embroidery floss is most commonly used. It comes in any color you want (and many more!) in small bundles, or skeins. A strand of floss is made up of six threads, or plies, twisted together. For a thick embroidered line, you can use all six threads. For smaller, more delicate work, you can separate the threads and use less. I use either six or three threads for most embroidery projects, and often one thread for hand sewing fabrics together. This saves on having to buy a whole spool of colored thread to match the fabric you're working with.

Standard cotton floss is most common, but there are also many specialty flosses available such as metallic, linen, silk, and gradient colors, which are fun to play with, as well as threads like crewel wool, which are used for specific types of embroidery.

When you unwrap a new skein of floss, it's a good idea to keep track of the number on the package. There are hundreds of different floss colors, and you may need to go back and get more to match later.

I use DMC brand floss and I've included the color numbers you'll need to make each project along with the instructions. If you use a different brand of floss, you can search online for a color conversion chart that will give you the equivalent numbers.

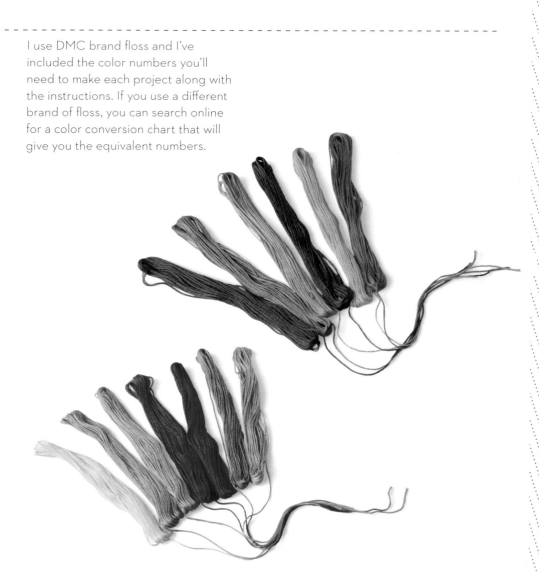

Needles

For most embroidery projects using regular six-ply floss, there is really no special size or type of needle you have to use to embroider with. All you really need is one with a sharp point and a hole, or eye, large enough that you can thread it easily. You will probably want a needle with a larger eye if you're using all six threads of floss, and one with a small eye if you're using three or less, or hand sewing with thread. I like to buy packs of several different sizes of needles so I have a variety to choose from. Keep a small pincushion close by to keep your needles from getting lost.

You'll want to use specific types of needles when stitching Sashiko and Crewel embroidery. Sashiko needles are longer and thinner than regular embroidery needles to allow you to make several running stitches at once. Crewel needles have extra large eyes that are easier to pass the thick wool thread through. If you have trouble threading your needle, try folding the end of the wool thread, pinching a crease, and passing the bend through the needle.

Embroidery Hoops

Although you can embroider some heavy, thick fabrics without a hoop, most fabrics will require one. Hooping your fabric will give you a tight, smooth surface to stitch on and prevent puckering. Embroidery hoops have two round frames that fit together and tighten with a screw. The frames hold your fabric tightly between them as you stitch on it. They come in plastic or wood, and in many different sizes. Plastic hoops are a good investment; they are sturdier than wood and will last a long time. You can use different-sized hoops for different-sized projects, but I've found a 6-inch (15.2 cm) hoop works well for almost anything.

Fabric and More

You can embroider on any fabric or material you can stick a needle through. The most common is quilter's cotton. Felt, canvas, denim, and satin are also great fabrics to embroider on. Try embroidering your clothes, dish towels, pillowcases, or any other fabric you find needing a little added interest.

You may not have thought about embroidering other surfaces besides fabric, but heavy paper, vinyl, thin plastics, and even wood can also be embroidered with a little creativity.

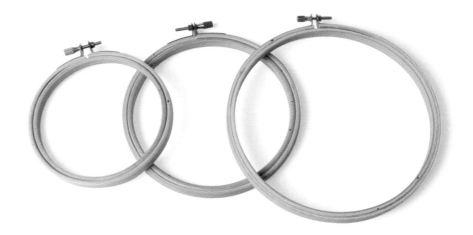

Stabilizer

When embroidering on stretchy or delicate fabrics such as T-shirt cotton or silk, you will want to use a fabric stabilizer. Stabilizer comes in many varieties. The type I use most is the tear-away paper kind with a sticky back. You can easily cut it to whatever size or shape you need, stick it onto the back of your fabric, and remove and reposition it if necessary. You will then stitch through the paper and fabric together. After you're done, just tear away the excess. For delicate fabrics, choose a water-soluble stabilizer that will simply dissolve in water when you're done embroidering.

Scissors

Any pair of scissors will do, but it's nice to have a small pair of sharp sewing scissors that you can keep with your embroidery floss and supplies.

Thimble

A thimble is nice to have when stitching heavy fabrics like canvas or denim. A leather or rubber one will make gripping and pushing the needle through the fabric much easier on your fingers.

Transferring Patterns

There are several methods for transferring embroidery designs and patterns to fabric. Different ways work better for different types of fabric.

Start by copying the pattern onto tracing paper or making a photocopy.

Light Method

The method I use most is tracing patterns on a light table or a sunny window. Tape your pattern to the table or window and secure the fabric on top so you can see the lines though it. My favorite tools for tracing pattern lines onto fabric are water-soluble fabric markers. These lines are easy to remove with water when you're done embroidering. An ordinary lead pencil will work too, although the lines may be more difficult to remove later. Just be sure you cover lead pencil lines completely with your embroidery. This method works best for lightweight, light-colored fabrics.

Carbon Paper Method

Another way to transfer patterns to fabric is by using carbon transfer paper. It comes in a variety of colors to contrast the color of fabric you're using. Place your fabric on a hard surface, place a piece of carbon paper face down on top of it, and your pattern on top of that. Trace the pattern lines with a pencil or other blunt object, such as a knitting needle. I use this method mostly for darker colored fabrics that marker lines don't show up on.

Iron-On Transfers

A third method is to make an iron-on transfer. You can do this by making a black-and-white laser print or photocopy of any design. Remember, especially if your pattern includes text, that you'll need to reverse the image before printing it because it will be backwards when you apply it to your fabric. Simply place the print on top of your fabric face down and iron it on. The lines will be permanent (though they may fade with washing or over time) so you'll want to cover them completely with your embroidery. It's a good idea to test this method on a scrap piece of fabric before using it on your project to see how long you'll need to iron and how dark the lines will become.

Tissue Paper Method

One more transferring technique is to trace your pattern onto thin paper (like tissue or tracing paper), pin the paper to your fabric, and stitch right through the paper and the fabric together. When you're done, just tear away the paper. This method works well for thick fabrics like felt, which can be tricky to transfer onto any other way.

Basic Techniques

After you've chosen your pattern and transferred it to fabric, you're ready to get to work!

Hooping Up & Stitching

First, stretch the fabric onto a hoop. Place the fabric over the inside frame and the outer frame on top of that, fitting them together. Tighten the screw and gently pull the edges of the fabric so it's tight.

Next, choose a color of floss, cut a length of about 12 inches (30.5 cm) long, and thread your needle. If you have trouble, try dampening one end of the floss and twisting it to a point. Tie a knot in the other end of the floss. One way to tie a knot is to wrap it around your finger, roll it off, and pull downward to tighten it.

Now, the fun part, start embroidering! Pull the needle and floss through from the back of your fabric until the knot catches. Now choose a stitch and follow the lines. When you finish a line or color section of embroidery stitches, or you get down to about 2 inches (5.1 cm) of floss, you'll want to tie a small knot on the back by slipping your needle under a stitch, looping it, and pulling it tight. Snip off the extra floss and start again.

You can work on your embroidery section by section, completing each area before moving on to the next one, or stitch everything you want to be in the same color before moving on to the next color.

When you've finished your embroidery, remove the fabric from the hoop and remove any transfer lines by rinsing it with water or hand washing it with a gentle detergent. Press the water out by spreading the fabric out flat or rolling it between two towels. When it's almost dry, iron it face down on a towel. This will remove any wrinkles but prevent crushing your stitches.

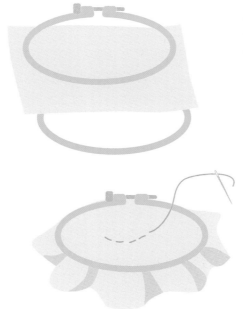

Sewing Stitches -

Mastering a few easy sewing techniques can open you up to a world of simple sewing projects. Here are a few techniques and special stitches used on the projects in this book.

HIDDEN STITCH

This is a nearly invisible stitch used to close holes in pillows or toys after they're stuffed. Fold the excess fabric in along each side of the opening and pin the hole closed. Thread a needle with thread matching the color of the fabric and knot it at one end. Bring the needle and thread through the fabric from the back at A and back down directly across the opening at B. Slide the needle along the inside of the fold and pull it back out at C, trapping the stitch inside. Reinsert the needle across from C at D, pulling the thread tightly. Continue stitching along the opening, closing up the seam. When you get to the end, make a tiny knot buried in the seam.

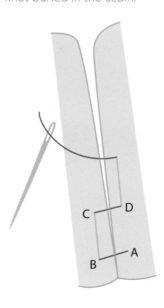

TOPSTITCH

Topstitching is done by hand or machine after the fabric pieces are sewn together and the project is turned right side out. Use a sewing machine or just sew a line of small Straight Stitches close together through both layers of fabric. Topstitching is usually done close to and parallel with an edge.

WHIP STITCH

Whip Stitches are a great way to add a decorative touch while joining pieces of fabric together along matched edges. You can also use it to hem the raw edge of a piece of fabric or alone as a decorative stitch. Use matching thread to hide your stitches or embroidery floss in a contrasting color to show them off.

Starting at the back or between two pieces of fabric, bring your needle and floss through at A. Bring the needle over the edge of the fabric and reinsert it from the back at B.

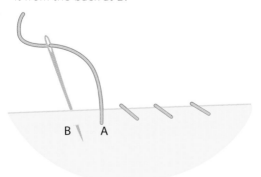

STAB STITCH

The Stab Stitch is a variation of the Running Stitch using very tiny stitches. It's most often used to attach a separate piece of fabric to your background fabric. Use thread matching the fabric or one thread from a strand of floss. Bring the needle up at A and down at B, 1/8 inch (0.3 cm) from the edge of the fabric. Continue stitching all around the edge.

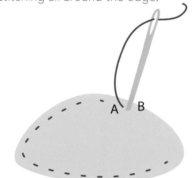

DOUBLE HEM

Your projects will look neat and professional with this hem. Just fold the edge of the fabric under twice, press, and stitch it in place using a sewing machine or a tight Back Stitch. To make a ½-inch (1.3 cm) double hem, fold the cut, or raw, fabric edge ½ inch (1.3 cm) to the underside and press. Now fold the edge under ½ inch (1.3 cm) again and sew along the top through all the layers of fabric.

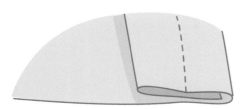

NOTCHING EDGES

When making projects such as pillows or stuffed toys, you will sew two pieces of fabric together with the right sides facing. Before you turn the fabric pieces right side out again, you will want to first "notch" the fabric around the seam so that the edges of your finished project look neat and smooth.

For curved edges, cut small, triangular pieces out of the fabric, cutting right up to, but not through, your stitched seam. Make notches ½ to 1 inch (1.3 to 2.5 cm) apart. The tighter the curve, the more notches should be cut. Cut corners off straight across as shown.

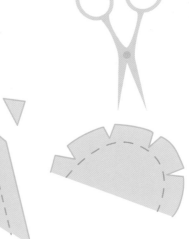

Stitch Glossary

Here are some common embroidery stitches that are used in various projects throughout this book.

Back Stitch

The Back Stitch is a nice, clean outlining stitch. Start with a small stitch in the opposite direction, from A to B. Bring your needle back through the fabric at C, ahead of the first stitch and ending at A. Repeat to make each new Back Stitch, working backward on the surface and inserting the needle at the end of the previous stitch.

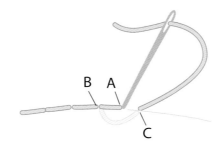

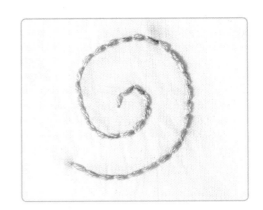

Blanket Stitch

The Blanket Stitch makes a great decorative border or edging. Make a loose, diagonal stitch from A to B. Bring the needle up again at C, catching the floss under the needle and pulling it tight to the fabric.

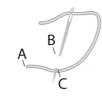

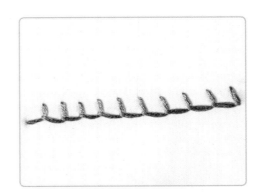

Chain Stitch

The Chain Stitch is great for a thick outline, but also works nicely as a decorative border. Pull the needle and floss through the fabric at A. Insert the needle back in at A, pulling the floss through to the back until you have a small loop on the front. Bring the needle back up through the fabric inside of the loop at B. Reinsert the needle at B, pulling the floss through to form a second small loop. Continue stitching loops to make a Chain. When you finish a row, make a tiny stitch over the end of the last loop to hold it in place.

To join a Chain Stitch circle, stop one stitch short of the first stitch, and slide your needle and floss underneath it at C. Then finish the last stitch, completing the circle.

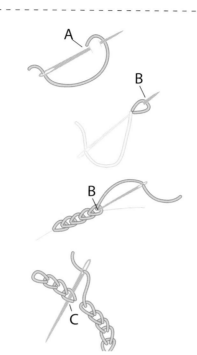

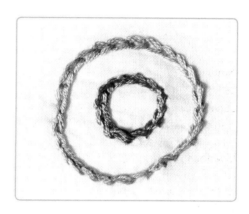

Fly Stitch

The Fly Stitch is an interesting decorative accent stitch and also makes cute flowers. Pair it with a Satin Stitch circle or French Knots to form the buds. Make a loose horizontal stitch from A to B. Press the loop flat to one side with your finger. Bring the needle back up at C, in the center of the first stitch. Return the needle at D, securing the first stitch to the fabric.

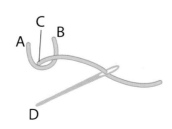

French Knot

French Knots can be tricky at first, but they are well worth taking the time to learn. Individually, they make great dot accents, or you can fill an area solidly with French Knots for an interesting texture. Bring the needle through the fabric at A. Wrap the floss around the tip of the needle in the direction shown, and reinsert the needle at B, right next to A. Pull the floss tight and close to the fabric as you pull the needle back through. You can make larger French Knots by wrapping the floss around the needle multiple times.

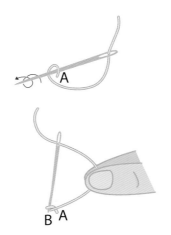

Lazy Daisy

The Lazy Daisy is the perfect way to make flower petals and leaves. You can use Satin Stitches or French Knots to make the flower centers. Bring your needle through the fabric at A and put it back down in the same spot, but don't pull the floss all the way through; leave a small loop. Now bring your needle back through the fabric inside the loop at B and back down at C, catching the loop at the top and securing it to the fabric. Repeat this stitch in a circle to make a daisy.

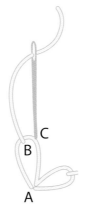

Long and Short Stitch

The Long and Short Stitch is used to cover large areas with a solid or blended color. Start the first row by making a stitch from A to B. Next, make another stitch right next to it from C to D, only half as long. Continue making a long stitch, then a short one to form the first row. Only the first row has both long and short stitches; the rest of the stitches will all be the same length. For the second row, make stitches just below your first row of stitches, filling in the spaces. Unless you're stitching a perfect square of Long and Short Stitches, they probably won't all be perfectly uniform, and that is just fine. Add a stitch here and there to fill in any gaps as you go along. Just keep your stitches all going in the same direction, and you'll have an evenly filled area when you're finished.

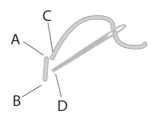

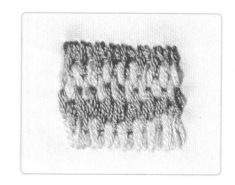

Satin Stitch

Satin Stitches are a lovely way to fill in small areas with smooth, solid color. Make a Straight Stitch from A to B. Make a second stitch right next to the first one from C to D. Always bring your needle up on one side and down on the other for best results. If you have trouble keeping the edges of your area even, first outline the shape with a tight Back Stitch or Split Stitch, and make your Satin Stitches over the top.

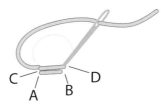

Scallop Stitch

The Scallop Stitch is a cousin to the Fly Stitch and Lazy Daisy and is made with the same basic technique. Scallop Stitches are also great for making flowers or leaves, or stitch several in a row to make a pretty border. Make a loose stitch from A to B and press it flat to one side with your finger. Bring the needle to the front of the fabric at C, inside the loop. Insert the needle at the outside of the stitch, at D, to hold it in place.

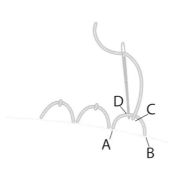

Split Stitch

Split Stitch lines are quick and easy to make, and they make great outlines. Make a small Straight Stitch from A to B. Bring the needle back up at C, splitting the first stitch in half. Continue making stitches and splitting them, to form a line.

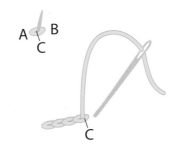

Stem Stitch -

The Stem Stitch is perfect for stitching curved lines or flower stems, which is how it got its name. Make a stitch from A to B, leaving the floss a little loose. Pull the needle to the front again at C, between A and B and just to one side. Pull the floss tight and continue to form a line of stitches.

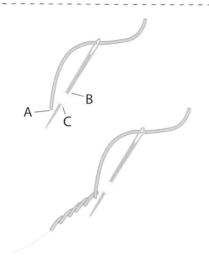

Straight Stitch -

The Straight Stitch is the most basic embroidery stitch. Just pull your needle through from the back at A, and push it back down at B. Straight Stitches can be any length, from a tiny dot to a line about ¼ inch (0.6 cm) long. Make several Straight Stitches one after another in a line to form the Running Stitch.

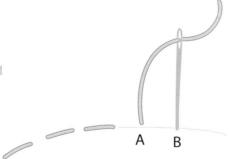

Variations

Keep the creative inspiration coming with these
extra patterns and variation ideas!

Variation for the
Candyland Apron
(page 34)

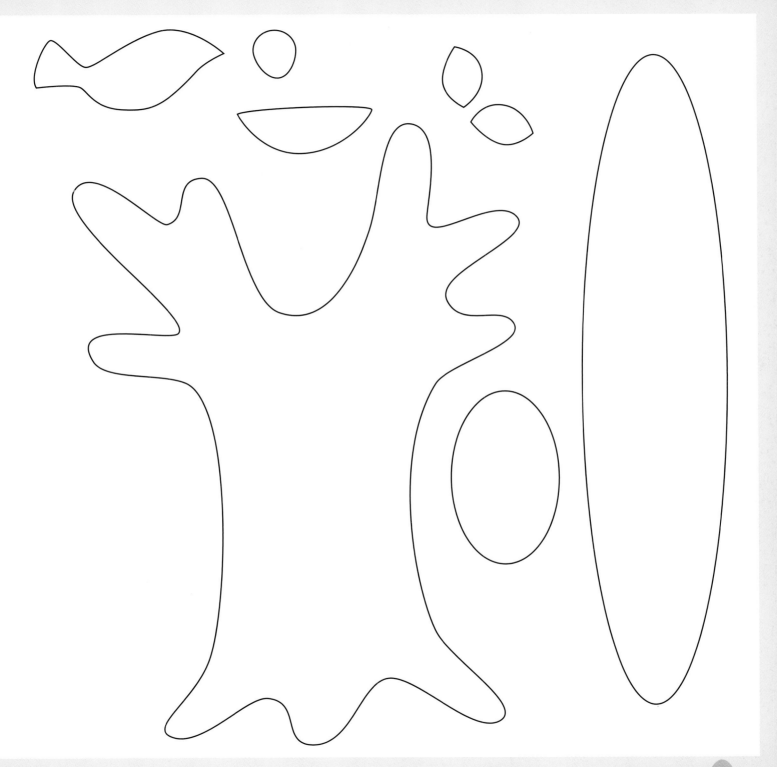

I'm NUTS over you!

Variation for the Owl Love
Paper Card

(page 44)

Variation for the Crewel
Peacock Messenger Bag

(page 60)
Enlarge 150%

Cross Stitch Alphabet for ABCs & 123s
Cross Stitch Bibs

(page 16)

Variation for the *Shisha Skirt*

(page 75)

Variation for the
Fancy Feathers
Throw Pillow

(page 93)

Extra Redwork Panel

(page 50)

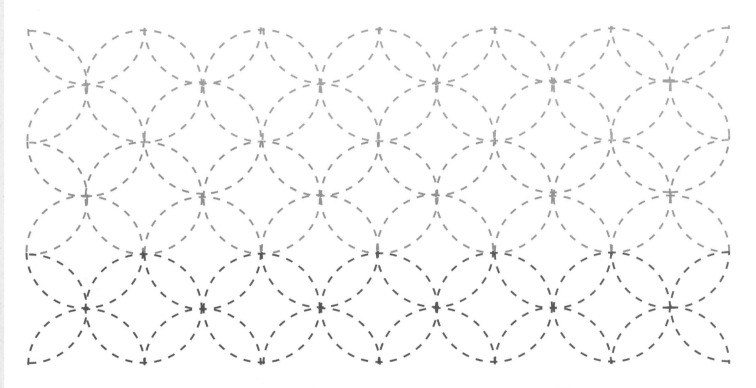

Variation for the Pond and Scales Sashiko Placemats

(page 70)
Enlarge 200%

padded flowers and bunny templates

wired leaves and ears templates

Variation for the Merry Mushroom Pincushion

(page 87)

About the Author

Aimee Ray loves all types of art and crafts and is always trying something new. Besides embroidery, she dabbles in illustration, crochet, needle felting, sewing, and doll customizing. Aimee's home is in Northwest Arkansas where she has a view of the Ozark Mountains from her backyard. She lives with her husband Josh, their baby son, and two big dogs.

Aimee has written two previous books of contemporary embroidery designs: *Doodle Stitching* and *Doodle Stitching: The Motif Collection*, and has contributed to many other Lark titles. You can see more of her work at www.dreamfollow.com and follow her daily crafting endeavors at www.littledeartracks.blogspot.com.

Acknowledgments

Writing my third book has been lots of fun, and I'm so thankful to everyone who has helped make it possible. Many thanks go to my husband, Josh, and my family, who always encourage me in everything I do. Thank you to my mom, grandmas, and creative aunties who were always making something when I was growing up, and instilled in me a love of crafting. Big thanks to my awesome editor, Amanda, and the team at CrescenDOH for helping to make this book perfect.

I'm inspired every day by so many people and great resources online, here are a few of the best:

www.inaminuteago.com
www.feelingstitchy.com
www.needlenthread.com
www.purlbee.com
www.woolandhoop.com
www.sublimestitching.com
www.thecraftytipster.com
www.carinascraftblog.wardi.dk
www.wildolive.blogspot.com

Index

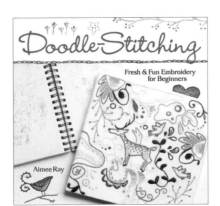